How United Methodists Share Their Faith

How
UNITED
*M*ETHODISTS
Share
Their Faith

Rodney E. **WILMOTH**

ABINGDON PRESS/Nashville

HOW UNITED METHODISTS SHARE THEIR FAITH

Copyright © 1999 by Abingdon Press.

This book is printed on acid-free paper.

Scripture quotations are from the Holy Bible: New Revised Standard Version, copyright © 1990 Graded Press. Hymn references are from The United Methodist Hymnal, copyright © 1989 The United Methodist Publishing House.

Library of Congress Cataloging-in-Publication Data

Wilmoth, Rodney E., 1937-
    How United Methodists share their faith / Rodney E. Wilmoth.
       p.   cm.
    Includes bibliographical references.
    ISBN 0-687-07584-X (alk. paper)
    1. Evangelistic work. 2. Witness bearing (Christianity) 3. United Methodist Church (U.S.)—Doctrines. I. Title.
    BV3790.W494 1999   99-32744
    248'.5'08827—dc21   CIP

99 00 01 02 03 04 05 06 07 08—10 9 8 7 6 5 4 3 2 1

MANUFACTURED IN THE UNITED STATES OF AMERICA

*This book is dedicated to Dr. Harvey H. Potthoff,
retired professor of theology at
Iliff School of Theology of Denver,
who helped me develop a faith worthy of sharing.*

Contents

Introduction

Now among those who went up to worship at the festival were some Greeks. They came to Philip, who was from Bethsaida in Galilee, and said to him, "Sir, we wish to see Jesus." Philip went and told Andrew; then Andrew and Philip went and told Jesus. (John 12:20-22)

IN THE GOSPEL of John, we are told of some Greeks who went to Philip and said to him, "Sir, we would see Jesus." The Bible says that Philip went and told Andrew, and then Andrew and Philip went and told Jesus. What would you do if a neighbor, family member, or someone with whom you worked were to ask you, "I would like to see Jesus." What would you say to them? What would you do? Would you bring them to church? Would you quote them Scripture? The disciples knew what to do. This book is designed to help persons share their faith so that others might know something of the power of Christ, which you experience in your life.

There are at least three books in me, and this is not one of them. Let me explain. Over the past several years I have been working on some book ideas. This book came about because Richard Peck, long time friend and editor of *Newscope*, tracked me down last summer on my Colorado vacation with the interesting and challenging invitation to write a book on the subject of how to share our Christian faith. I was immediately intrigued by the assignment and quickly accepted the challenge. I did so for two reasons.

First, to speak to the reluctance some persons have in sharing their faith.

For some people faith sharing is difficult, and there are good reasons for this.

1. Some persons may not yet be certain of their own faith.

This is understandable. Many people are a part of the Christian faith but may not all be at the same place in their faith journey. There may also be those whose lack of certitude may be caused by the fact that they have not yet experienced Christ personally. Hopefully, this book will assist persons in developing their faith to the point that they might be able to articulate it and share it with others.

2. Some persons have negative feelings about sharing their faith.

The driving motive for persons to share their faith in much of the eighteenth and nineteenth century was: 1) to save souls from eternal damnation and to secure their place in heaven; 2) to preserve the institution of the Christian church; and 3) to secure the expansion and preservation of our national life.[1]

3. Some persons may not be certain just how to share their faith in a pluralistic and inclusive environment.

Faith sharing today is much different than it was as recently as 25 years ago. Today, Christians in this country find themselves surrounded by many non-Christians. Christians today live in a world that is highly secular, multicultural and multi-religious. How do we as Christians today share our faith with conviction while, at the same time, being respectful of those whose faith is just as significant to them?

A. Some persons feel that faith is a private matter.

Two men were discussing a funeral they had just attended for a close friend of theirs. One expressed surprise to the other by saying, "I didn't know George was a Methodist!" The way some Christians move about, one would think that are trying to keep their faith a secret.

To be certain, a part of our faith journey is private, but that is only half the picture. The faith that we read about in the Bible was as much public as it was private—maybe even more so. Look at the way Paul shared his faith. Look at the way Jesus shared the faith as he spoke to specific individuals. John Wesley, the founder of Methodism, certainly knew the value of a blended faith both private and public. Wesley's Aldersgate experience was certainly private and personal, but very quickly the spiritual awakening that took place in his life became the very centerfold of his preaching. The very core of Wesley's beliefs and convictions had to do with the public side of his faith, where daily he witnessed to a faith that had the power not only to transform individuals but vast societies as well.

B. Some persons have been turned off and even offended by the evangelistic techniques of the electronic church, the TV evangelists, or by those who come door to door to witness to their faith.

This, too, is understandable; however, we need to consider what might happen if everyone took this position. The word *gospel* means good news. The Gospel of Jesus Christ would have ended long ago if there had not persons willing to share their faith with others. It is important for us to realize that you may very well be the only "gospel" someone hears. This leads to the fifth reason why some persons are reluctant to share their faith.

C. Some persons do not know how to go about sharing their faith.

Hopefully this book will help persons learn how to share their faith in a way that will enable others to experience the presence of God in their life the way you experience that presence. Each chapter deals with a specific guideline designed to help individuals in the sacred task of sharing their faith.

Second, to speak to the reasons for sharing our faith.

There are essentially three reasons for sharing our faith.

1. It fulfills the Great Commission.

Now the eleven disciples went to Galilee, to the mountain to which Jesus had directed them. When they saw him, they worshiped him; but some doubted. And Jesus came and said to them, "All authority in heaven and on earth has been given to me. Go therefore and make disciples of all nations, baptizing them in the name of the Father and of the Son and of the Holy Spirit, and teaching them to obey everything that I have commanded you. And remember, I am with you always, to the end of the age." (Matthew 28:16-20)

The Gospel of Jesus Christ (the Good News) is to be shared throughout the world not just by missionaries in foreign lands, but also by folks just like you and me. We should share our faith with our neighbors, as well as persons with whom we work, in our car pools, and in our classrooms.

2. It fulfills the mandate of the Methodist movement.

On his 85th birthday, Wesley paused to reflect on his life and ministry. He wrote in his journal for June 28, 1788:

It is true I am not so agile as I was in times past. I do not run or walk so fast as I did; my sight is a little decayed; my left eye is grown dim, and hardly serves me to read; I have daily some pain in the ball of my right eye, as also in my right temple...and in my right shoulder and arm, which I impute partly to a strain and partly to the rheumatism. I find likewise some decay in my memory in regard to names and things lately passed, but not at all with regard to what I have read or heard twenty, forty, or sixty years ago; neither do I find any decay in my hearing, smell, taste, or appetite (though I want but a third...of the food I did once); nor do I feel any such thing as weariness, either in traveling or preaching; and I am not conscious of any decay in writing sermons, which I did readily, and, I believe, as correctly as ever.

During the next week, the elderly Wesley kept the same energetic pace, which had marked his ministry for more than fifty years. He preached sixteen times, in twelve different towns. He attributed his extraordinary spiritual keenness and physical strength to God's power at work in his life, the vital prayers and support of his brothers and sisters in the faith, and his disciplined life.[2]

Born June 28, 1703, John Wesley spent a lifetime sharing his faith. He openly shared both his doubts as well as his beliefs. Out of that Wesleyan tradition come the guidelines for sharing our faith.

❏ Sharing the Christian faith does not mean that we are trying to persuade others to adopt a point of view, but rather to point to the person of Jesus Christ.

❏ We are called to introduce people not to a plan or proposition, but rather to the person who brings health and wholeness.

❑ Jesus Christ does not call people to a religion; Jesus Christ calls people to himself and to his reign.

❑ People give their lives to God not because God sends them a tract or an advertisement, but because God sends Jesus Christ.

❑ Our belief in the nature of God leads us to the conclusion that the best witness we can make is to tell persons of the living God whose presence is felt everywhere and is especially seen in the Christ.

3. It fulfills the Gospel in bringing hope and meaning to those who are searching.

Our General Board of Discipleship tells us that persons between 17-24, one of the largest segment of our population, have no Christian memory. This means that we have a lot of people who do not know the creeds of the church. They know very little, if any, about the stories of the Bible. Yet they are searching for values, traditions, rituals. What a wonderful opportunity for those of us in the faith, who have been blessed and enriched because of our walk with Christ, to share that faith with others!

This task may be somewhat intimidating simply because, for many of us, it has not been an ordinary part of our religious experience. We have tended to leave the business of sharing the faith with the "professionals," like the clergy or those who have been trained for this particular ministry. As the church prepares to move into the next millennium, we are discovering that the best evangelists are not the professionals, but rather the men, women, youth, and even children who make up our congregations.

George Hunter III, of the School of World Mission and Evangelism, recently wrote an article describing why he feels the area of evangelism ought not to be left to ministers. He began by reminding us that the Great Commission was directed to the whole Christian community, which at that time was a lay movement. His primary concern is that the pastor often lacks the credibility of most pre-Christian people.

> Indeed, the pastor may never have enough credibility with about half the unchurched population. The day you get ordained, you lose half of unchurched people. They now perceive you as a paid propagandists for the institutional church; it is your job to commend the Christian religion and recruit members for the church. With those people, lay people have much more credibility. That is why, in evangelism, the "amateurs" outperform the professional, two to one![3]

The purpose of this book is to help persons discover the gift of sharing their faith with others. We have been empowered by God to carry out this ministry of faith sharing. Jesus promised his disciples that power would be given to them to fulfill his ministry and mission in the world. "But you will receive power when the Holy Spirit has come upon you; and you will be my witnesses in Jerusalem, in all Judea and Samaria, and to the ends of the earth" (Acts 1:8).

There is a direct correlation between the Holy Spirit and sharing our faith. The Holy Spirit energizes our efforts to witness. The Holy Spirit also guides us in our efforts to share our faith with others. The Holy Spirit also motivates us to risk sharing our faith. The Holy Spirit prepares others so that they will be receptive to our witnessing.

Appreciation is given to Jim Jackson, senior minister of Chapelwood United Methodist Church, for his ideas that helped me develop the guidelines for this book.

Hopefully this study will provide the reader with some helpful insights as to not only why sharing our faith is important, but also how we might do it with biblical and theological integrity.

Guideline # 1
Make certain you have made
a commitment to Jesus Christ.

Chapter 1

More Than Shrine Visiting

"I am obliged to bear witness because I hold a particle of light,
and to keep it to myself would be equivalent to extinguishing it."
—Gabriel Marcel

Isaiah 49:1-17, John 1:35-42

BILL BRYSON, AUTHOR of *The Lost Continent: Travels in Small Town America*, tells of traveling to Hannibal, Mo., to visit the boyhood home of author Mark Twain. He said the house was a "trim, white-washed house with green shutters, set incongruously in the middle of downtown." It cost two dollars to walk around the site. Bryson found the house to be a disappointment.

He writes: "It purported to be a faithful reproduction of the original interiors, but there were wires and water sprinklers clumsily evident in every room. I also very much doubt that young Samuel Clemens' bedroom had Armstrong vinyl on the floor or that his sister's bedroom had a plywood partition in it."

He said that the house, which is owned by the city of Hannibal, attracts some 135,000 visitors each year. But Bryson was disappointed that he was not able to actually go inside the house. "You look through the windows," he says. "At each window there is a recorded message telling about each room."

As he proceeded from window to window he asked another tourist, "What do you think of it?" The friendly stranger replied, "Oh, I think it's great. I come here whenever I'm in Hannibal—two, three times a year. Sometimes I go out of my way to come here." Dumbfounded, Bryson replied, "Really?" "Yea," answered the tourist. "I must have been here twenty, thirty times by now. This is a real shrine, you know!"

As the two of them continued walking, Bryson asked his last question of the man. "Would you say the house is just like Twain described it in his books?" "I don't know," said the tourist. "I've never read one of his books."

Visiting his shrine but ignoring his books. That is a pretty good description of a lot of Christians today. They are quick to visit the shrine but seldom, if ever, read the Book. This is also a pretty good description of the relationship many people have with Jesus. They faithfully attend worship but seldom manage to apply the teachings of Jesus in their daily living. It seems like there are plenty of people searching for the historical Jesus, but not many these days who are willing to follow the living Christ.

The writer of the Gospel of John paints a fascinating picture of a rare moment in the lives of several persons. Jesus had just been baptized by his cousin John. Later he came into the presence of John and his disciples, and John explained to them that Jesus was the Lamb of God who takes away the sin of the world. Two of John's disciples immediately began following Jesus. One of the two was Andrew.

Focus your attention on Andrew, for he was the first disciple to "discover" Jesus and join him. His response is the key in this whole matter of shrine visiting. Andrew was a follower of John the Baptist, but when Jesus was pointed out to him, Andrew embarked on what would be the beginning of a life-transforming experience.

Not everyone is like Andrew. Too many persons settle for just visiting the shrine. But that was not enough for Andrew. He wanted to know about this person Jesus. He was not willing to settle for just shrine visiting. Maybe that is one reason why some folks never get past the shrine; they fail to recognize any personal relationship with the Christ.

In the Bible we find very little about Andrew, yet what we do know tells us volumes. We see that he was willing to settle for second place, as he would spend most of his life being in the shadow of his brother Simon Peter. For example, when Jesus climbed the Mount of Transfiguration, he took his faithful three: James, John, and Peter. Andrew was not included.

We also know that Andrew was apparently willing to settle for the fulfillment of minor tasks—tasks that he did well. You may recall that it was Andrew whom Jesus asked to go ahead of the group on the day of the triumphal entry into Jerusalem. He was instructed to untie a colt and tell its owner that his Master needed it. Not a big task in the grand scheme of things, but a critically important one for the completion of Jesus' mission.

What is worthy of note is what Andrew did in response to meeting the Christ. His response has much to say to a people who live in a world where Jesus is either a non-entity or a major stumbling block for the thinking Christian. Notice what Andrew did when Jesus was pointed out to him. It was far more than just shrine visiting.

First, Andrew Follows Jesus

I am struck by the way John tells the story. He simply says that Andrew and his friend just followed Jesus. At that moment Jesus did something that was so predictably characteristic; he turned around and asked Andrew, "What are you looking for?" (1:38). Don't miss the significance of that seemingly innocent question, for in that brief moment we see of the magnitude of God. Jesus' turning around is a symbol of divine initiative, as it is always God who takes the first step. It is God who finds us, not the other way around.

A few years ago, a popular religious bumper sicker often found on the cars of the theologically challenged read, "I've Found It!" In truth, it is not we who find God, but God who finds us. Now that is something to shout about! I believe it was Augustine who said, "We could not even have begun to seek for God unless God had already found us." This says it well!

"What are you looking for?" A two-thousand-year-old question that is still pertinent today. What are you looking for? Security? A position that is safe? Money enough to take care of all contingencies? Military power and clout that will enable us to rest easy in a world dealing with conflict? Are you looking for a career that will provide power, prominence and prestige? Or are you looking for an opportunity to render service consistent with your capabilities?

Perhaps Andrew's reason for following Jesus might very well be our own. When John the Baptist said, while pointing to Jesus, "Here is the Lamb of God who takes away the sin of the world" (John 1:29), that was enough for Andrew. Maybe he followed because he desperately wanted someone who would not only take away the sins of the world but his sins as well. Is that not one of the reasons why we follow the Christ today? We follow in the hope that Jesus will turn around and ask, "What are you looking for?" And we can say, "We are looking for acceptance, love, forgiveness, a new beginning, and a greater understanding of the meaning and purpose of life."

The world is filled with people who are looking for individuals who will give them that sense of meaning and purpose. The tragic life of Edgar Allen Poe is an example. He died in alcoholic discouragement at the age of forty. Apparently he could never find someone who would give his life meaning. Both his mother and father had died in Richmond, Va., when he was two years old, and he was reared by his godparents. Poe's gambling debts at the university became so large that his godparents turned away from him. He decided to marry his high school sweetheart only to discover that she had already married someone else. He went to New York City. To finance his gambling and drinking problems, he was now selling his famous stories for only fifty to one hundred dollars apiece.

This alcoholic young man was looking for someone who could give his life some meaning. He heard that his old sweetheart had been widowed, and she agreed to marry him. But on his way home, someone gave him a glass of sherry, and he never made it. His life was a tragedy. Edgar Allen Poe, who left all of us richer for his literary works, never found that one person who could give meaning and purpose to his life.

We really do not know much about Andrew, except that he apparently saw something in Jesus that was lacking in his own life. So, he silently began to follow Jesus, the Lamb of God who takes away the sins of the world.

The Second Thing Andrew Does is to Tell Jesus That He Wants to Go to His Home

"Where do you live, Rabbi?" Andrew was not asking Jesus for his street address. His blunt question was much deeper than that. "Who are you, really?" "What are you about?" Apparently, where Jesus lived was of importance to Andrew. Andrew had some deep issues to discuss, and evidently no mere conversation on the street would be sufficient. Andrew knew that the best way to get to know a person was to be in their home. At home you learn some things about people that cannot be gained in any other way. "Where do you live, Rabbi?" And Jesus said, "Come and see."

Many modern day Christians wonder why their faith lacks depth. Perhaps it is because we settle for just shrine visiting rather than going into the home of Christ. Too many of us are quite content to follow without getting too close. There is nothing that will add depth to the Christian experience more than recovering a sense of being in the presence of Christ. Andrew did not want to know Jesus from a distance; he wanted to experience Christ in his own life.

We live in a time that is 2000 years removed from this meeting between Jesus and Andrew. How are people today able to meet and experience Christ? We often settle for letting our doctrines or our creeds accomplish this for us, but that is so impersonal.

One of the great preachers of an earlier generation was Henry Sloane Coffin, who on one occasion preached from this text of John's gospel. He ridiculed Webster's definition of the word *kiss*: "A touch or caress with the lips, often with some pressure and suction . . . ." Coffin noted that while the description is accurate, it is of very little value to a mother who kisses her child or two lovers who thrill to each other's presence.

Doctrinal statements, creeds, articles of religion—all of these have their place, but if we are depending on them for a personal relationship with Christ or for our religious experience, then we are going to come up empty. John Wesley was reported to have said, "Do not explain your God to me; tell me how you experience God in your life." I doubt if very many persons over the years have ever been led to Christ through a doctrinal statement or creed. Christ comes to persons not in statements but to those who, like Andrew, are willing to make their home with him.

"Where do you live, Rabbi?" Jesus answers, "Come and see." Rabbis often ask, "Do you want to know the answer to this question, or do you want to know about the solution to this problem? Come and see, and we will think about it together." When Jesus invited Andrew to "come and see," he was inviting him not only to come to his home and talk, but to come and find the things that he alone could open to him. John finishes this paragraph with the words: "It was about four o'clock in the afternoon" (John 1:39).

In nearly forty years of Bible study, I have come to the conclusion that there are no unnecessary words in the Bible. Every word is there for a purpose. In John's own way he is saying this was a classic moment in the spiritual life of Andrew, so much that the exact time was noted. Very similar is John Wesley's famous Aldersgate experience when he received a new inspiration at a prayer meeting in London on May 24, 1738, "at about quarter til nine", when he said that he felt his heart "strangely warmed...."[1]

Such a pattern is not unusual. Before John Newton gave to the world the wonderful hymn Amazing Grace, and became a noted English cleric, he said of himself, "I hated life and life hated me." But that all changed when someone placed into the hands of this "wreck of a man" a copy of Thomas Kempis, *The Imitation of Christ*. That was John Newton's "four o'clock" moment of his life, and six years later, struggling to find inner peace, he would come to love life and life began to love him. When he entered into the ministry, he wanted people to know that he had a marvelous secret to share and went all over England sharing that secret in his preaching. Toward the end of his life (1807), he insisted on preaching every Sunday even though he was nearly blind and needed an assistant to stand with him in the pulpit! One Sunday, during his sermon, he repeated the phrase, "Jesus is precious." His assistant whispered to him, "Sir, you've already said that twice." Newton replied, "Yes, I've said it twice, and I'm going to say it again." Then, at the top of his old voice, he sang out once more, "Jesus is precious!"[2]

We will probably never know what all was said while Andrew was in the home of Jesus. But whatever it was, it made a life-transforming impact on him. "It was about four o'clock in the afternoon", and Andrew's life would never be the same again.

The Third Thing Andrew Did Was to Run and Tell His Brother, Simon Peter, "We Have Found the Messiah!"

There are those who believe that the ultimate of religious experience is to be able to say, "I've found it!" or "I'm saved!" These exclamations are powerful if—and I repeat, IF—those who say such things see them as a beginning point rather than an ending point. Too often folks stop there, and when they do they commit a form of biblical heresy, for the biblical imperative is that once we have experienced Christ in our lives, like Andrew, we must go out into the world and tell someone else!

Andrew becomes the patron saint of sharing the faith and the good news with others by introducing them to Jesus. Actually, there are at least three times when Andrew takes center stage. The first one is here, in which he tells his brother about Jesus. The second is when Andrew brings the boy with the sack lunch of loaves and fish to Jesus (John 8-9), and the third incident is when Andrew brings the inquiring Greeks into the presence of Jesus (John 12:22). It was Andrew's joy to bring others to Jesus. Andrew stands out as the one whose only desire was to share the good news. Here is someone with a true missionary's heart. Having himself found the friendship of Jesus, he spends the rest of his life introducing others to that friendship.

What I am suggesting here is that there is something more to religion than just shrine-visiting. In his book *The Unfinished Task*, Stephen Neill quotes from one of the participants at the World Council of Churches, who said that every person needs to have three conversions: to Christ, to the church, and to the world. First, an individual finds him or herself challenged to surrender to the recognition of Christ as the supreme Master. Second, a person uncovers the reality of the Christian faith in the shared fellowship and mystery of the church. And third, one finds him or herself overwhelmed by the sorrows and sufferings of humanity and then discovers Jesus of Nazareth as the pattern and inspiration for a life of service. That fits Andrew to a "T" and truly best defines what we can experience in our own religious faith.

Andrew's going out and telling his brother about meeting with the Messiah is symbolic of the kind of action needed by the contemporary Christian today. It is not just verbal. Anytime you respond to a mission need in your congregation, you are like Andrew. Anytime you contribute to the work of The United Methodist Church, you are demonstrating the kind of action required whenever we meet the Christ. When you leave church, you have an opportunity to leave as Andrew did, going out into the world with words and deeds that can bring healing and hope.

Laid upon each and every one of us is the necessity to bear witness to the mighty power of Christ in our own lives. Once we know Christ personally, it is impossible not to talk about him whenever the opportunity presents itself. Is there not an irresistible urge to make that good news known to others? John Bunyon, the author of *Pilgrim's Progress*, said that when he came to the full realization that Christ was now his friend and savior and Lord, he went home singing a hymn at the top of his lungs. "I knew not how to contain myself," he wrote. "I felt I could have spoken of his love to the very crows that sat upon the plowed lands before me."[3]

When Christ becomes real and personal to us, it is most difficult to suppress what is the greatest thing that ever hap-

25

pened to us. We want everyone to know the good news. We do this first because of the joy within us, and second because we realize that it is a part of our responsibility as Christians to share our faith. Gabriel Marcel said it well when he wrote, "I am obliged to bear witness because I hold a particle of light, and to keep it to myself would be equivalent to extinguishing it."[4]

When Wilfred Grenfell was a student at Oxford, he attended a tea one afternoon. As he was talking with another student, Grenfell raised the question as to what Christ's attitude might be about a particular subject. The dean of the college overheard the conversation and got him aside and said, "My dear Grenfell, we never speak of these things [meaning Christ's attitude] in general conversation." Grenfell could not help it. He spoke of Christ and Christ's way of life for the rest of his life whenever he was given an opportunity.

Grenfell lived an amazing life. He practiced medicine among Labrador fishermen and Eskimos. He built hospitals and nursing stations and established cooperative stores, agricultural centers, schools, libraries, and orphanages, all in the name and for the sake of Christ. He witnessed for Christ not only by his dedicated life, but also through the many books he wrote about his life as a medical missionary. He bore witness by word and deed to the saving and life-changing power of Christ. He could not help it; it was all too good to keep to himself. Wilfred T. Grenfell was like the man who once said about Christ, "Now that I know him, it is my job to make him known." That was the spirit of Andrew. He wanted to know Christ, and once he knew him, he wanted to make him known to others. According to the Bible, the first thing he did was to go and tell his brother, Simon Peter.

It is not enough for us just to go and visit the shrine. We have to read the Book. We have to appropriate the life of Christ in all we say and do. When that happens, we, like Andrew, will go and tell the world.

26

Discussion Questions

1 Why is it important for individuals to have a personal relationship with Christ?

2. If you were to talk to someone who was not a part of the Christian faith, how would you go about helping that individual develop a personal relationship with Christ?

3. Do you feel it is important to make a personal commitment to Christ before you can effectively share the faith with someone else?

4. What does your belief about Jesus tell you about the nature of God?

5. What role do doctrinal statements, creeds and articles of religion play in religion today?

6. Share whatever experience you have had in making a witness to your faith.

7. Would you say that the average Christian would see as their role to make Christ known to others as did Wilfred T. Grenfell?

Guideline # 1
*We are called to love persons, not
change persons.*

*The late Donald Soper stated it well:
"We must begin where people are,
rather than where we would like
them to be."*[1]

Chapter 2

Look Up to the Earth

Mark 10:13-16

COLONEL CHARLES DUKE was a member of the *Apollo 16* crew who drove the lunar buggy on the moon. He described his feelings as he emerged from the space module and took his first tentative steps through the dust of the lunar surface, experiencing the sensation of weightlessness.

He said, "I looked up at the earth and stood silent for a moment, drinking in the wonder and being conscious of a flood of new feelings as I looked up from afar at our world." He said at first it seemed incongruous to look up at the earth. "After all," Duke said, "we are accustomed to looking up at the moon." He said that as he stood looking up at the earth and marveling at its beauty, that for some inexplicable reason he lifted his open hand toward the earth and suddenly realized that the palm of his hand completely blocked the view of the whole world. He stood there, almost spell-bound, for a considerable time, allowing the power of that experience to work its way throughout his mind and emotions and soul.

Duke said that for the first time in his life, he began to understand the oneness, the wholeness, the singleness of the world; and further said that from that moment on, his perception of the world as a community had been dramatically and permanently altered. For the first time he felt that it was possible for people, for all of God's children, to live together in singular world community where they could reach out and touch each other and communicate with each other.[2]

Like Colonel Duke, we know we can block out the entire earth with the palm of our hand, and often do so. It is so easy for us to hold up our hand and block out those groups and individuals who do not look nor think like us.

One of the reasons why some are reluctant to share their faith is because they are not certain how to do it in an environment that is not Christian, highly secular, multicultured and multireligious. Today we live in a world that is very pluralistic, and sometimes quite biased, prejudiced, and narrow in its view of others.

We also live in a world filled with people who have no awareness of the Christian faith. How do we as Christians witness to our faith to those whose religious values and understandings are far different from ours, such as Muslims and Jews, just to name two?

How do we share our faith with those who really want nothing to do with religion, especially the Christian religion? Is there a way for us as Christians to be able to witness to our faith in such a way that we are accepting of different views and understandings?

Most of us were taught as Christians that Jesus Christ is the Savior of the world. He is not just another religious prophet, but in fact, the Son of God. We have also been taught that God chose to reveal God's self in the form of Jesus Christ.

But we are now living in a different day. We are living in a world where some folks have a lot of misgivings about who we are as Christians. We live in a world filled with people who consider Jesus, his birth, death, and resurrection as a questionable myth. In addition to that quandary, our world is becoming more and more the global village in which we are more conscious of differing cultures and religious traditions. If we adamantly affirm that Jesus Christ is the Savior of the world, we quickly set ourselves not only apart, but also in a divisive relationship with many other persons living in the global village. Does this mean that we need to change or modify our understanding of who Jesus is? I think not. But what is required is for us to consider three critically important issues.

Issue Number One:
Strive to learn how to both interpret and share the Christian faith in such a way that is not exclusive.

Several months ago I attended a gathering of clergy in Orlando, Florida. The group was made up of clergy from all over the nation and from all over the theological spectrum. There were mainline denominations represented, plus many non-mainline. Included in the non-mainline were conservative, fundamentalists, pentecostal, and charismatic representatives. Some of the pastors in attendance served churches with memberships exceeding thirty thousand members!

This particular group came about several years ago largely due to the encouragement of Dr. Robert Sculler of the Crystal Cathedral in Garden Grove, California. Dr. Schuller is held in high regard with this clergy group. After he spoke to the group, Dr. Schuller said that he would be happy to answer any questions anyone might have.

At that point, one of the clergy said, "Dr. Schuller, I read recently that you gave an address to a national gathering of Muslims. Why did you speak to them and what did you say?" There was something about the question that implied that a Christian would have no reason to speak to such a group.

Robert Schuller, in his usual open and direct manner, said, "I was honored to speak at their national gathering. I talked about what Muslims and Christians have in common. That in many ways, we both come from the same roots and that we could accomplish much by working together focusing not on our differences but on our similarities." And then, sensing the uneasiness with the question, Dr. Schuller said, "Let me tell you about a book I'm reading now. The author said, 'Don't be surprised if when you die and go to heaven, you will meet people there who have never heard of Jesus Christ.' "

A hush fell over the nearly eighty clergy persons. The hush was broken by a pastor of one of the largest churches in America saying, "But Dr. Schuller, the Bible says in the Gospel of John that 'no one will come to the Father except through me.' " Dr. Schuller looked at him for a moment and said, "Yes, my friend, I know that's what John said, but I'm not so sure John knew everything."

That was an important comment to make. I doubt if everyone present especially liked what Dr. Schuller said, but it was the right thing to say given where we are in our world today. Christians who feel that they have exclusive membership in heaven may be in for a real surprise. My congregation has often heard me say, "If you have Jewish neighbors and you're not getting along, you had better work on improving the relationship because in all reality, they will be with you in heaven!"

There is even a deeper issue here regarding the danger of touting a faith that is not always appreciated for some of its actions. For example, at the Schuller Institute in January 1999, Dr. Schuller told the nearly three thousand participants that on his worldwide television broadcast, he is very careful in his use of the words *Christianity* and *conversion*. He said that there are too many people in our world who are experiencing horrible actions by so-called Christians.

Dr. Malone Dodson, senior minister of the Roswell United Methodist Church in Roswell, Georgia, was in our church to preach for one of our Wednesday evening Lenten services. He told of a Bosnian family that his church has helped to relocate. He said that the family members are Muslim, and the only thing they know of Christianity is from the Christian Serbs who killed two of their children, attempted to rape the mother and wife, and slashed open the husband who fell on his wife to protect her from being raped. Such actions make it difficult to speak about Jesus Christ as the Savior of the world, and that as followers of Christ we want to convert all persons to Christianity, when such atrocities are taking place in the name of Jesus Christ.

Issue Number Two:
Remember that Jesus is a process, not a product.

In order for us to share our faith in a multicultural and multireligious world, we need to remember that Jesus is a *process*, not a *product*. This is not in any way to diminish the personhood of Jesus, but it is, however, an understanding that Jesus is not a product that we sell. The most effective way of sharing our faith with those who are of a different culture and/or a different religious background, is to tell people of the Christ we know and experience. Share with others what difference Christ has made in your life, or in the lives of others. This is certainly in keeping with our Wesleyan heritage. Look again to John Wesley's Aldersgate experience in which he felt his heart strangely warmed. Why did he feel his heart strangely warmed? Let Mr. Wesley tell us:

> In the evening I went very unwillingly to a society in Aldersgate Street, where one was reading Luther's Preface to the Epistle to the Romans. About a quarter before nine, while he was describing the change which God works in the heart through faith in Christ, I felt my heart strangely warmed. I felt I did trust in Christ, Christ alone for salvation, and an assurance was given me, that he had taken my sins, even mine and saved from the law of sin and death.[3]

There are more and more people around us at school or at work or in our neighborhoods who are starving spiritually because they have not found that inner experience Christ can bring. Each of us is given a wonderful opportunity to share with others who and what Christ is to us. The following steps will help insure that our faith sharing is more than selling a product.

❏ Tell how having Christ as your personal savior has enabled you to feel whole and complete.

❏ Tell how having Christ at the very center of your being enables you to live a full and abundant life, free from self-imposed barriers and limitations.

❏ Tell how having Christ in your life has enabled you to become an advocate for the powerless, the marginalized, and the dispossessed of our society.

❏ Tell how having Christ in your life has helped you to overcome fears and anxieties, thus freeing you to experience the full potential of your life.

❏ Tell how having Christ in your life has helped you rediscover the moral compass of your life.

❏ Tell how having Christ in your life has given you a new sense of purpose and direction.

Such testimonies are very compelling and will do far more to gain you a hearing in today's world than insisting that unless persons accept Jesus Christ as their Lord and Savior they will never enter heaven nor will they be with God. It is possible that the passion of one's faith does not have to be divisive.

Issue Number Three:
Remember that all persons are children of God.

Psychologist Carl Rogers, famous for his non-directive counseling, made a statement regarding acceptance that is worth repeating:

> I have come to believe that appreciating individuals is rather rare. I have come to think that one of the most satisfying experiences I know, and also one of the most growth-pro-moting experiences for the other person, is just fully to appreciate an individual in the same way that I appreciate a sunset.

> People are just as wonderful as sunsets—if I can let them be. When I look at the sunset, I don't find myself saying, 'Soften the orange a little on the right hand corner, and put a bit more purple along the base, and use a little more pink in the cloud color.' I don't do that. I watch it with awe, as it unfolds. I like myself best when I can experience my staff members, my son, my daughter, my wife, myself, in this way—appreciating the unfolding of life.[4]

Alex Shoumatoff has written a book entitled *The Mountain of Names*. The Mountain of Names is a vault built by the Mormon Church within a mountain near Salt Lake City, Utah. There on microfiche and microfilm are recorded more than a billion names—all members of the human family. The

Mormons tell us that they now have enough genealogy to confirm that everyone is kin. Now there is a sobering thought! We are all related to each other. When you come to the Communion table, you kneel not in isolation, but with a relative.

I have attended only one family reunion in my life. It was held on a beautiful Sunday afternoon on the front lawn of the family farm where my grandfather and his two sisters were born in Athens, Alabama. There were many kinfolk gathered on that lawn, most of whom I had never met.

I was standing in the lemonade line behind an elderly woman and a young girl of about twelve years of age. The girl turned to the woman and said, "Grandma, who are all these people?" Her grandmother said, "Why, honey, these are all your kinfolk." With that the little girl looked at me in a most incredulous way and said in a sarcastic tone of voice, "Am I related to *you*? It probably did not make her day when I said yes, but in that moment two strangers realized that they were related to one another.

Members of my congregation often hear me say, "I'm in sales, not management." People will ask me to pray for good weather for the church picnic, and I remind them that I am in sales, not management. I truly believe this. We are not asked to help manage the universe. If we are trusting and faithful Christians, we will leave the managing to God. Our task is sales. That is to say, our task is to share our faith in such a way that we are not trying to "sell" Jesus to anyone, for Jesus is not a product. Jesus is a process which we "sell" to others by sharing how the Christ makes a difference in our lives and everything our lives touches. In that sense we share our faith with all persons.

Jesus is our model for sharing our faith. He was willing to share his life and ministry with all persons as evidenced by his conversations with persons like the woman at the well, or Roman officials, or persons who were trying to entrap him. Even the stories Jesus told reveal his inclusiveness to all persons; stories dealing with lepers, prodigals, Samaritans, and many others deemed as social outcasts. Jesus' style was to love not change.

One of the great Christian missionaries was E. Stanley Jones. He spent most of his life working among the Hindus in India. He was there on a mission for Christ, and he never wavered in that mission. It is important to note that he lived among the Hindu people in such a way that he was dearly loved by them. In fact, many of the conversions to Christ for which he was responsible came from people who were so moved by the love they saw in him and the respect they received from him that it made his passion for Christ all the more attractive and credible and compelling. The model of E. Stanley Jones can serve us well, not in some far off place, but right here where we live.

We are living in a global village that is rapidly shrinking while at the same time rapidly expanding in diversity. In sharing our faith it is important to know that we do so in partnership with God. Once we have been faithful in sharing with others what our Christian faith means to us, we trust that God will enable the seeds of our faith to take root and grow.

Discussion Questions

1. Do you as a Christian feel like you are in the minority when at work or at school?

2. Do you believe that Jesus Christ is the *only* means of salvation?

3. List ways in which we hold up our hand and block those who are not like us and do not think and believe as we do.

4. List ways in which you can share your faith with persons whose religious orientation is different from yours.

5. Does it help to think of Jesus as a *process* rather than a *product?* If so, how?

6. List what you feel are the most difficult challenges in sharing your faith.

7. Do you feel that you are a partner with God when sharing your faith? If not, discuss ways in which this partnership can be felt.

8. How would you go about sharing your faith with someone who is a good person, yet sees no need for religion?

9. Looking back on this past week, what opportunities were provided for you to share your faith with someone? Did you make use of those opportunities? If the answer is yes, share that information with the group. If the answer is no, ask yourself, "What kept me from sharing my faith?"

10. Prepare a list of all of the actual settings during the course of a typical day where you are given an opportunity to witness to your faith. Plan what your course of action might be to share your faith in the days to come.

Guideline # 3
*Remember that the object of faith
sharing is not to win an argument
but to win a person.*

Chapter 3

Called to Be an I-Witness

Luke 24:35-48

A FICTIONAL EXECUTIVE wanted to inspire his employees. He went throughout his building putting up signs reading, "Do It Now!" Sometime later, someone asked him how his staff reacted to the signs. He said, "I wish I had never put them up." "Why?" asked the friend. "Didn't anyone respond to the signs?" "Oh, yes," he said. "That was just the trouble. They did! The cashier skipped off with five thousand dollars, the head accountant eloped with the best secretary I ever had, three clerical secretaries asked for a raise, and the factory workers all voted to go on strike!"[1]

Maybe there are some things that ought not to be done right now, but on the other hand, when it comes to matters of faith, responding right now might be the best approach.

In this chapter we want to take a look at Luke's account of the final resurrection appearance of Jesus. This passage is critical because it achieves three important objectives. First, it speaks to the doubters. Luke shows us that Jesus is not a figment of the disciples' collective imagination. Jesus invites persons to touch him. Second, Luke says that Jesus wants to make certain the disciples have the story straight. Jesus goes over the details, explaining to his disciples how he had fulfilled all of the promises and predictions that had been made about the Messiah in the Old Testament. The final objective is the most important. Here Jesus clearly establishes the mission for the early church. He gives the disciples the task to go about preaching repentance and forgiveness in Christ's name to all the world and they are to do this as witnesses of all that has been said and done.

Many Christians are uncomfortable with the word *witness*. For some it conjures negative feelings. We have been around folks who have made us feel uncomfortable by their witnessing to the faith. Or we feel uncomfortable with the notion that we need to share our faith with others. After all, we reason, faith is a personal and private matter, and we should not be forcing our faith on someone else.

Such feelings are understandable, for many of us have experienced negative witnessing. Having said that, however, we come back to the biblical imperative that it is our task as Easter people to help others know something about the Christ who is in our midst. It is never enough for us to know about the birth, life, death, and resurrection of Christ. We are called by God to tell the world about the gifts of repentance and forgiveness brought to us by Christ.

Someone may say, "How can I be an witness to all of this? I was not around at the time of the disciples. I did not see any of this." While we may not have been an eyewitness to the events of the past, it is possible for us to be an I-Witness, for we have experienced what Christ talked about to his disciples. Today we are called to be I-Witnesses to the faith.

Called to Be an I-Witness to a Faith That Is Forgiving

In his play *An Inspector Calls*, J. B. Priestly tells of a detective from Scotland Yard who is investigating the suicide death of Eva Smith. Those persons supposedly closest to Eva Smith apparently knew very little about her. A relative is not certain she knows Eva until she sees some pictures. Similar reports were made from each member of the family. No one seemed to know much about Eva Smith, nor did they care. Perhaps each had contributed to her decision to commit suicide. Perhaps we need to ask, "How many people have we passed who might have found life if we had been willing to share the potential power of love and caring that is found within us?"

There are many persons in our midst who are carrying heavy burdens. Some of those burdens might be there because of something they have done. Imagine what you might be able to do for them by sharing with them your personal experience of a forgiving Christ.

Called to Be an I-Witness to a Faith That Is Active

The story is told of a very boring, negative, and judgmental guest preacher who had been invited to preach at the Yale University chapel. He took the word *Yale* as his test, and let each letter serve as a point of his sermon. He said that the "Y" stood for "youth." He talked for more than twenty minutes on youth, railing against the youth of today. The letter "A" stood for "ambition," which prompted another twenty minutes of lamenting that no one had ambition today. The guest preacher said that the letter "L" stood for "loyalty," and he spoke on loyalty for twenty boring, negative minutes. By the time the preacher got to the letter "E," he had already preached for over an hour, but that did not stop him. He went on for twenty more boring, negative minutes dealing with "energy."

41

At the conclusion of the service, the choir and the guest preacher recessed down the center aisle. On the last row, the preacher saw a student on his knees praying fervently. The preacher was thrilled that his message had so inspired this Yale student. He stopped and asked the young man what he had said in his sermon that so moved him "to such fervent prayer." The student answered, "I was just thanking God that I go to Yale and not the Massachusetts Institute of Technology! That would have taken eleven hours and twenty minutes."[2]

God did not give us a boring, negative faith, but rather an active faith, filled with excitement and enthusiasm. Each of us is given an opportunity on a daily basis to be an I-Witness to such a faith. Imagine the joy you could bring to someone by sharing your uplifting faith. It may very well be the most important gift you give to someone else.

Called to Be an I-Witness to a Faith That Is Involved

Edgar J. Helms was born on January 19, 1863. His mother wanted him to be a minister. The biographer stated, "He showed a disinclination for exclusively spiritual teaching, and a propensity for action." Apparently Edgar Helms did fulfill his mother's wishes. He graduated from Boston University School of Theology and was ordained an elder in The Methodist Church. At one point in his ministry he was appointed by the bishop to an inner city mission where he ministered to poor immigrants, persons involved with crime, and persons suffering from unemployment.

In the midst of this situation, Edgar had an idea for collecting unwanted clothing and household goods. He also had a dream of providing employment for disabled persons to help relieve the poverty condition that caused so much pain. His idea became a reality. Today it is known as

Goodwill Industries, which is now found in thirty-eight countries outside of the United States. No less than thirty thousand people a day cross over the thresholds of the Goodwill Industries. Today it is the largest non-profit organization of its kind in the world, meeting the vocational needs of disabled people.[3]

Edgar Helms was an I-Witness to a faith of involvement. He was willing to "do it now" in terms of his understanding of the faith. Sometimes the best way we can share our faith is not so much by what we say but by what we do.

Called to Be an I-Witness to a Faith That Is Triumphant

From all biblical evidence, it would appear that we worship a God who wants us to be happy. This happiness is not in the giddy sense, and it is certainly not in the sense that everything is all right, but God wants us to feel whole and complete. Happiness brought about by a sense of fulfillment. This suggests that our happiness is not to be found in our situation but in our attitude. When we feel good about ourselves we are more confident and positive. When we achieve this state, we will be of greater service to God and to one another. Such feelings do not always come easily.

She was just thirteen years old. She was poor and hungry and destitute, and she was on her own. The only world she knew anything about was the ghetto of New York City. To survive she did what other young girls had to do; she sold her body for sex.

After a few years, while waiting for her next "appointment," she was watching television. She watched a religious program where a minister was preaching a sermon. The minister said some things that really got to the girl. He talked about self-esteem and personal dignity, about living and the beautiful life that God created for us. The girl knew she had never experienced any of that beauty in her life. She had no self-esteem, and she did not feel that she had any dignity in her existence. The girl was so deeply moved by this sermon that she did not keep her appointment.

The next morning, she stood on the banks of the Hudson River and looked across to New Jersey. She was now twenty-five years old and had never been out of the ghetto, much less out of New York City. As she stood there on that riverbank, she felt God calling to her and offering her a new life if she would have the faith to risk.

Later that day she scraped together enough money to purchase a one-way bus ticket to California, leaving everything she had ever been behind. The outcome? Today this young woman has a master's degree in social work and is now working for the City of Los Angeles in one of their public assistance programs. She is helping other young women move to a new life. Because she became an I-Witness to a faith that is triumphant, she is now helping others to know the joy she had found.[4]

Called to Be an I-Witness to a Faith That Is Healing

In Port Hope, Canada, there is a monument erected to a man who was not a leading citizen. He was a poor, unselfish, working individual who gave most of his life and energy to help those who could never repay him.

The monument is erected to Joseph Scriven who was born in Dublin in 1820. As a young man it seemed that he would achieve success, for he was a person of high ideas and great aspirations. He was engaged to a beautiful young woman who had promised to share his dream. But on the eve of their wedding her body was pulled from a pond into which she had accidentally fallen and drowned. Young Scriven never overcame that shock. Although he graduated from college and embarked on a career, he began to wander in an effort to forget his sorrow. His wanderings took him to Canada where he spent the last forty-one years of his life. He became a very devout Christian and, in time, through the healing of his faith, was led to serve the poor, the sick, and the homeless, often for no wages.

It was not known that Mr. Scriven had any poetic gifts until a short time before his death. A friend, who was sitting with him in his illness, discovered a poem he had written to his mother in a time of sorrow; he had apparently not intended for anyone else to see it. His poem was later set to music and it has become a much-loved hymn that many of us have sung from childhood:

> What a friend we have in Jesus,
> all our sins and grief to bear!
> What a privilege to carry
> everything to God in prayer.
> O what peace we often forfeit,
> O what needless pain we bear,
> all because we do not carry
> everything to God in prayer.

Joseph Scriven became an I-Witness to a faith that heals. We, too, can become an I-Witness to that kind of faith. A faith that is

> Forgiving
> Active
> Involved
> Triumphant
> Healing

There are many persons who are struggling with life and death issues. Those of us who are part of a worshiping community can share our faith because we are I-Witnesses to what our faith can accomplish.

Discussion Questions

1. List the reasons why you think it is difficult for persons to witness to their faith?

2. Do you feel that your faith and your relationship to God would be of help to others? If so, why?

3. Do you think there is enough emphasis in preaching about encouraging persons to be an I-Witnesses for their faith?

4. What would be helpful for you to feel comfortable in being an I-Witness for your faith?

5. Do you feel that sharing one's uplifting faith could bring joy to others?

6. Can you think of someone who would benefit from your sharing your faith with them?

Guideline # 4
Tell your story.
It is virtually impossible to share
your faith without telling your story.

Chapter 4

Moving from Telling the Story to Being the Story

Acts 3:12-19 and Luke 24:35-48

THERE IS NO darkness quite like the darkness of despair. The darkness of dashed dreams can be overwhelming, leaving persons without any sense of hope.

That must have been something of the atmosphere in the upper room where eleven disciples gathered after the crucifixion of Jesus. The upper room held some wonderful memories, but all that was over. These disciples had run there to hide. They had been with Jesus during his entire public ministry. They had heard him tell his marvelous stories and had listened to his powerful sermons along the Sea of Galilee. These disciples had listened to the crowds cheering as Jesus entered Jerusalem. They had believed in Jesus and that the promise of the ages would be fulfilled. Now, brokenhearted, the disciples had fled. These once strong giants of the faith had been reduced to fear. Terrified by life itself, they gath-

47

ered in the upper room, surrounding themselves by darkness and doubt.

Just at that moment two persons from Emmaus came bursting into the room. They were filled with excitement. They had just seen the Lord! Just as the two men were beginning to explain how Jesus appeared to them during the meal, all of a sudden, Jesus appeared in the room!

Was this magic? Was this some sort of an apparition or an illusion? Jesus said, "Why are you frightened, and why do doubts arise in your heart?" Jesus proceeded to show the disciples his hands and feet, inviting them to touch him. Jesus then asked for food. The disciples were not seeing a ghost. Ghosts do not get hungry. This was Jesus' way of saying that he was in their midst. It was too good for these men to believe at first, but when they did, their lives were changed. That is so often the way it is whenever we encounter the risen Christ.

The late Loren Eisley was not only an archeologist and an anthropologist, but he was also a very significant writer. His roots were in my home state of Nebraska. Eisley's in-laws were members of Trinity United Methodist Church in Lincoln, Nebraska, which I was privileged to serve. Although I never met Loren Eisley, I have been greatly influenced by his unseen presence.

A member of my congregation who was a personal friend of Loren Eisley gave me a copy of a story Eisley had written called "The Magician" in which he shared an autobiographical account of an event that changed his life. He said that every person sooner or later meets the magician who will change his or her life. He said that he met his magician when he was fifty years old.

Eisley explained this life-changing incident. It happened in the old Pennsylvania Railroad Station in New York City. As Eisley started to go down a flight of stairs, he saw a man. It turned out to be his teacher and former colleague, who had been dead for a decade, standing at the bottom of the stairway.

As Eisley began to descend the stairs, his former colleague came up the stairs and turned. Eisley almost stumbled and fell when the man turned to him. His heart pounded as he stared at the man. When the two men met each other on the stairs, Eisley opened his mouth to say his name, but no sound came out. The man looked right past him without any recognition, continued up the stairs and out the door to be lost in the crowds of New York City.

Whether Eisley saw a ghost or an illusion, or whether the man was a clone of his former friend, Eisley does not know. He acknowledges that he will never be able to solve that mystery. On his trip back to Philadelphia, however, Eisley discovered the meaning of that unusual experience. He had been at his administrative job at the University of Pennsylvania for too long. It was time to get back to the work of anthropology and archaeology for which he had been trained. After meditating on this possibility, Loren Eisley went back to his desk at the university and wrote a letter of resignation.

The life of Loren Eisley had been completely changed by that mysterious encounter, much in the same manner that Jesus' appearance in the upper room altered the lives of the disciples forever. In this chapter I would like for you to consider what the disciples did when they encountered the risen Christ. It could very well be that their experience could be our experience as well, helping us in the art of sharing our faith with others.

Notice How They Moved from the Position of Doubt to One of Faith

We should not be too surprised by the disciples' doubting. After all, they had seen the Crucifixion, a form of Roman torture that no one had been known to survive. However,

Jesus suddenly appears in their midst! Were they hallucinating? Was this a ghost? Then the uninvited guest spoke to their unbelief. He was real and he was alive!

The Bible says that the disciples "in their joy... were disbelieving" (Luke 24:41). This phrase makes sense because Jesus' appearance was simply too wonderful to be true. How often we are like the disciples. We think of all those times we disbelieved for joy. Something was too good to believe; we struggled with our doubts. In fact, our doubts, perhaps, kept us from fully experiencing some of life's great moments. Because of this we search for those opportunities to move from doubt to faith.

Sometime ago I was invited to be the guest speaker for a district conference in the panhandle of Nebraska. I was scheduled to speak on a Sunday afternoon, which presented some logistical problems because I had to be at my own church in Omaha to preach that Sunday morning. The district committee told me that arrangements had been made for me to fly to McCook, Neb., on G. P. Express.

Now up until that time I had never heard of G. P. Express. Doubts were already beginning to settle in as I suspiciously wondered why any airline, except TWA, would be referred to by its initials. I was assured that it was a very fine commuter airline.

My doubts continued to rise when I was not able to find the G. P. Express ticket counter at the Omaha airport. I finally found the counter located in a very remote area of the airport. My doubts continued to rise when I saw the size of the airplane and heard the ticket agent ask me how much I weighed!

My doubts were not removed when I discovered that the ticket agent was also the pilot as well as the co-pilot and navigator. After learning this news, I full expected this multitalented man to tell me that he was also CEO and chairperson of the board of G. P. Express.

The only other passenger scheduled for the flight was a man who often had visited our church. When he heard me begin to verbalize some of my doubts, he intoned, "Padre, aren't you the one who quotes Jesus saying, `I am with you always?'" I said to my friend, "That is not what Jesus said. He said, 'Lo, I am with you always.'"

When the plane finally was airborne I discovered that the Lord was with us because the plane never did get very far off the ground. I could read the newspaper headlines people were reading while sitting out on their patios. The plane just barely flew above the trees and water towers. The flight turned out to be a wonderful way to see Nebraska.

Just as I was beginning to enjoy my low-flying flight across Nebraska, the plane developed engine trouble and our pilot announced that we would probably be landing somewhere before we reached the airport. I quickly scanned the horizon and asked in a doubtful voice where we would be landing. The pilot, who did not seem to be the least bit concerned, pointed down at a highway, "Either on the highway or over there in the cornfield."

It was at that moment that I realized what the letters G. P. actually stood for—great panic! While there was an element of panic, it quickly passed away because of the pilot's calm demeanor. He was absolutely unflappable. I watched him skillfully handle the controls, which enabled him to baby that small aircraft all the way to the nearest airport, where he put the plane down on the runway with a very smooth landing.

It was then that I discovered that the pilot, who was also the ticket agent, navigator, and co-pilot, was also the mechanic. It was Sunday afternoon and there was no mechanic on duty, so he worked on the plane himself. Within an hour the plane was up and flying, and I made it to my destination almost on time. I did not realize it at the time, but upon later reflection I realized I had moved from a position of doubt to one of faith because of that pilot.

Doubts and fears were riding high for the eleven disciples as well. There certainly was not much faith in their lives. Their faith had been spent on Good Friday when their hopes and dreams had been dashed as Jesus was crucified. The disciples must have felt terribly abandoned. But what turned all of that around? It was the encounter they had with the risen Christ, when they saw Jesus and shared bread with him.

Somewhere I remember reading a story by Leo Tolstoy, the great Russian writer, that told of a czar and czarina who wished to honor the members of their court with a banquet. The royal couple sent out invitations and requested that the guests come with the invitations in their hands. When they arrived at the banquet, the guests were surprised to discover that the guards did not look at their invitations at all. Instead the guards examined the guests' hands.

The guests were curious to see whom the czar and czarina would choose as the guests of honor to sit between them at the banquet. Amazingly enough, an old scrubwoman who had worked to keep the palace clean for years was chosen. The guests were flabbergasted. As the guards escorted her to her seat of honor, they declared, after examining her hands, "You have the proper credentials to be the guest of honor. We can see your love and loyalty in your hands."

Those discouraged, despondent disciples moved from doubt to faith because they saw in the hands of Jesus his never-failing love and presence.

Notice How Each Disciple Realized That They Had Been Called Upon to Share Their Faith

Clearly our task and calling is to tell the story. As the hymn says, "To tell the old, old story of Jesus and his love." But our task and calling goes beyond just telling the story. As I read the Scriptures, it becomes clear to me that these disciples did more than tell the story; they, in fact, *became* the story. They became the living testimony and to what they saw and heard.

Therefore, our task and calling is to become the story. In each and every age, women and men are called upon to share their faith, not only by the telling of the work of Christ, but also by the *doing* of the work of Christ. We share our faith whenever we minister to the needs of the world, wherever they are. We share our faith whenever we are willing to champion the causes of justice, truth, and decency. We witness to our faith whenever we stand tall in moments of conflict.

Our history is rich with persons who not only told the story, but also became the story. One such person was Sister Thea Bowman who met the risen Christ and spent much of her life not just telling the story, but being the story. She was a Roman Catholic nun, the granddaughter of a slave, and the daughter of a physician who was not allowed to practice medicine in the hospital of his hometown in Mississippi.

Shortly before her condition became worse, Sister Thea was invited to speak to the National Conference of Roman Catholic Bishops. It must have been quite an event. She began by asking them, "Do you know what it means to be black and to be in the church today? I want to tell you what it is like." She stood back from the microphone, standing there with great dignity—quiet for the longest time. Then she began to sing "Sometimes I feel like a motherless child a long way from home."

At the end of her speech, in which she talked about the Roman Catholic Church becoming more inclusive of all peoples, two hundred and fifty bishops stood and held hands, swayed from side to side, and sang "We Shall Overcome." Someone said that if Thea Bowman is nominated for sainthood, that will be the miracle they will mention in her behalf!

Notre Dame University planned to give Sister Thea the highest medal of honor to be given by that university at their commencement, but she was not there to receive the award. She died of cancer in 1990, a few weeks before the commencement. When the school awarded her the medal posthumously, they read some of the words that Sister Thea's students had often heard her speak: "Be black. Be white. Be man. Be woman. Be priest. Be laity. Be single. Be married. But be one in Christ."

I tell you this story because I want you to know that Thea Bowman was not born into the church. She was converted to Christianity. She was converted because she saw Jesus Christ lifted up by Roman Catholic nuns and priests in her Mississippi hometown.

At the age of fifteen, Sister Thea joined the Franciscan Sisters of Perpetual Adoration because, as she told the reporters the day she spoke to the bishops, "I was impressed by the courage and the witness of priests and nuns who made an effort to lift up Jesus in that town, and I decided to join them."[1]

What Does This Mean for Modern Day Disciples?

I asked my bishop, John Hopkins, Episcopal leader for the Minnesota Annual Conference, to read my manuscript of this book. He is a great believer in encouraging persons to tell their own story. As he said, "Sharing your faith is really telling your story." Almost all of us have a story we can share of how our faith either helped us personally or helped someone else.

After it is all said and done, there are really just two reasons why we share our faith or tell our story. First, to do so enables you both to claim your story and to appreciate what God has done in your life. Here, Bishop Hopkins has a good word for us: "If your story doesn't have any angels in it, don't put them in!" He says this as a way of demonstrating the value that we do not have to make our story "religious" in order to share our faith. Second, we share our faith or tell our story because we want others to know the workings of God's grace. As Bishop Hopkins says, "Sharing our faith is not so much a duty as it is a gift!"

This book is dedicated to my seminary professor of theology Dr. Harvey Potthoff. I dedicated it to him because he helped me to see the oneness of all of life, that all of life is whole and not fragmented into parts. Sacred and secular are one; science and religion are one. He enabled me to fashion a faith that allowed me to appropriate all of life's experiences into a meaningful pattern. This gift has made it possible for me to be open to all the wonderful ways we can see and experience the glorious acts of salvation. It has also made it possible for me to see the presence of the living Christ in all of life.

This powerful thought intersected with my life many years ago when I took our two small children to a parade in downtown Omaha. We arrived in good time to get choice curb-side standing. Even though there were thousands of people lining the parade route, I began to feel the presence of someone who was just a little too close. Turning to my side, I discovered the source of my uneasiness. A man of the streets, standing next to me, was hovering over my children. I shall never forget his appearance. His glasses were very thick. He was wearing a seersucker shirt buttoned right up the middle, leaving the top and bottom wide open. If the pants were his, he had lost a lot of weight, for they were gathered at the waist and held up by a rope.

I tried to wedge myself between the man and my children but was not having much luck. About that time, several clowns from the parade came skipping over to my children with some little handout. My children began jumping up and down with joy, and the man hovering over them was laughing with them and now had his hands on their shoulders. I was most uncomfortable and somewhat annoyed.

Once again I tried to step between my children and this man but was unsuccessful. When another group of clowns came over our way, my two children once again began jumping up and down, and now the man was no longer hovering over them with his hands on their shoulders, but had managed to stand between them. My discomfort and annoyance now turned into fear and anger.

Then, all of a sudden, a calming sense came over me. In those few moments I looked at the man and my two children. He wasn't hurting them. He was doing nothing inappropriate. I began to see this man in a different light. I no longer saw him as an intruder, a threat, or a stranger, but rather as a human being who probably had a family but lost them along the way. I pictured him as a grandfather who no longer had contact with his grandchildren and for those few moments was enjoying being part of a family. Once again the clowns came over our way, and I shall never forget looking over to my children and this man and seeing all three of them jumping up and down with excitement and laughter, with my two children reaching up and holding on to his hands. It was one of life's holy moments.

When the parade was over, I turned to greet my new friend. I wanted to thank him for being with my children. I wanted in some way to thank him for "saving" me, but when I turned to greet him, he was gone. The city that had coughed him up seemed to have swallowed him, and I never saw him again. On the way home, my daughter Jennifer asked, "Daddy, did you know that man at the parade?" I answered, "No, honey, I never saw him before in my life." But I have to tell you that I have always wondered if I had not seen the Christ.

In the beginning I was a Methodist by birth, but no longer. Today I am a United Methodist by choice. The theology of John Wesley is what stirs and excites me so by blending and balancing issues such as piety and social action. Christian being and doing are two vitally important issues which must always been viewed together.

Not long after I went to St. Paul United Methodist Church in Omaha, I was asked by the Salvation Army if I would be willing to give the invocation at a banquet honoring one of my members, the late J. D. Anderson. It was a huge event, large enough that they brought in the general of the Salvation Army from Chicago as the speaker.

He began his remarks by saying that he loved the opportunity of speaking to a captive audience because it gave him an opportunity to explain his uniform. I remember thinking to myself, *This is going to be a trip!* It was, and a delightful one at that. He really did not explain his uniform, but he did explain the two brass buttons on the lapels of his coat. With his thumb under his right lapel, he pointed the brass button "S" to the audience and said. "This button is very important. It tells the world that I have been saved. I realize that might not mean a lot to some of you here today, but it means everything to me. It means that for me Jesus is my personal Savior." Then he put his thumb under his left lapel, pointed the left brass button along with the letter "S" towards the audience, and said, "This button stands for service." And then he got quite serious and said, "Friends, I have been saved for one reason and one reason only: to serve! Quite frankly, I grow very weary of some of my Christian brothers and sisters who go through life pointing to the right button of being saved and have not clue what the left button is all about!" To his testimony I say, "Amen!" Remember, you may be the only Christ some will ever meet, and you may be the only Bible some will ever read.

The risen Christ is alive in us; the risen Christ is alive in his church. God is doing mighty things these days. May you experience the risen Christ in your life so that you can move from doubt to faith. May you not only be able to *tell* the story, but may you be able to *be* the story!

Questions for Discussion

1. How do you handle your doubts?

2. What does it take to overcome your doubts?

3. When have your doubts turned to faith?

4. When have your doubts kept you from experiencing great moments of life?

5. What are some "disbelieved joys" for you?

Guideline # 5
Know your audience.
Tailor what you say to a person.

Chapter 5

One Size Does Not Fit All

John 4:1-30

AS ONE READS the conversations Jesus had with people, it appears that he allowed the individual with whom he was speaking and their situation to determine the direction of the conversation. This principle is most vividly seen in John's account of Jesus visiting with the woman at the well. He spoke both to her situation in life and the condition of her soul. What Jesus said to her was quite different from what he said to the lepers, for example, or to what he said to the blind beggar whose eyesight had been restored. Clearly, Jesus did not have a "one-size-fits-all" approach in his efforts to encourage persons to seek a higher level in life. In each case Jesus tailored his comments to fit both the person and their situation.

This is an important principle when it comes to sharing our faith with others. It is important to note that there are major differences in people and their needs. For us to be effective in witnessing to our faith, we need to know our audience.

Knowing Our Audience

For the first time in our history, we now can identify at least three different generations. Each generation is quite different and unique. The following table helps us to see the identifying characteristics of each of the three generations. Noting these differing characteristics will provide helpful guidance in sharing our faith with others.

BUILDERS	BOOMERS	BUSTERS
52 + years	33-51	14-32
Commitment to Christ	Commitment to Christ	Commitment to Christ
Commitment to church	Commitment to relationships	Commitment to family
Program oriented	People oriented	Community oriented
Money to missions	Money to people	Money to causes
In-depth Bible study	Practical Bible study	Issue-oriented Bible study
Loyalty to denomination	Loyalty to people	Loyalty to family
Minister out of duty	Minister for personal satisfaction	Minister to meet needs
Support missions	Support big causes	Support local causes[1]

Many Busters, and Boomers as well, are taking another look at the church. They are viewing it with a careful and critical eye. Knowing your audience will help you share your faith in a way that will be meaningful not only for the other persons but for yourself as well.

Witnessing to Our Faith in the Next Millennium

The desired goal, of course, is to be able to share our faith with all persons.

But we have a window of opportunity the likes of which we have not experienced before in our lifetime. We have an opportunity to share our faith with a segment of our society who has very little knowledge about the Christian faith. According to our General Board of Discipleship, we now have the largest segment of our society of 17 to 24 year-olds who have no Christian memory. They know very little if anything about creeds, prayers recited from memory, or stories from the Bible. These persons are often referred to as Busters, Gen X'ers, or PreChristians. People like Lyle Schaller, Herb Miller, and Bill Easums are telling us that if a person in that age category comes to a Sunday morning worship service, there is a good chance that is the first time they have ever attended a worship service.

One of my colleagues in the ministry, Dr. Nelson Griffith, a retired American Baptist minister, tells of a young woman who came up to him following a funeral he had just conducted asking if she could get a copy of the poem he read. He said he wasn't sure what she was referring to because he had not read any poem. She said, "You know, the poem about a shepherd walking through a valley." Nelson said she was referring to the Twenty-third Psalm; she had not known that he had read from Scripture. It is very clear that we need to decipher the gospel for the next generation.

Responding to the Great Spiritual Hunger

When I first arrived at Hennepin Avenue United Methodist Church, I was told about a survey that had been taken in our area prior to my arrival. Hennepin Avenue United Methodist Church is located in the most densely populated part of the Twin Cities. A high percentage of that population is made up of Busters. While I never saw the actual survey, the results were quoted to me on several occasions. As many as ninety percent of the persons interviewed said they were interested in seeking a spiritual life. However, approximately eighty percent of those persons said it would never occur to them to look to the church for that spiritual life. When I shared those figures with our bishop, John Hopkins, he thoughtfully replied, "Back in the 1950's a lot of churches were filled with persons who knew very little about spirituality. Today we have a lot of people who are interested in spirituality but know very little about churches."

We live in a spiritual universe, and our task is to share the reality of the faith. Three years ago we invited Dr. Lauren Artress, author of *Walking the Sacred Path*, to come to Hennepin Avenue United Methodist Church to help us establish our labyrinth ministry. We saw this ministry as an entry point for those persons outside the church searching for spiritual values. I shared the survey figures with her and she explained that was why she was devoting so much time and energy to helping churches establish a labyrinth ministry. "There is a spiritual revolution going on in our society," said Dr. Artress, "and I am fearful that it will take place outside the church."

Her fear is justified. Busters are looking for spiritual values; their search often takes them in all the wrong places. We who are in the church have a faith that many outside the church are longing to have, but unless we are willing to share that faith, it will go unheard. Targeting our audience and learning how to share our faith with persons in this age group can be truly rewarding. The following table can help us understand how our search for spirituality can take us on different paths.

How Generations Differ in Terms of What People Are Looking for in Their Faith Journey

	BUILDER	BOOMER	BUSTER
Speaker	Orator	Communicator	Sojourner
Content	Reason	Truth	Experience
Logic	Deductive	Inductive	Raw
Role	Pious	Professional	Personal
Language	Clear	Picturesque	Graphic
Attitude	Optimistic	Overly Optimistic	Concerned
Talk About	Faith	God	Jesus
Offer	Moral lessons	Advice—10 steps	Hope—Jesus[2]

Keep in mind that the average Buster wants to know the following three things:

Is God accessible?
What difference does it make?
Are you for real?

Understanding the Concerns of Busters

Before we attempt to share our faith with the Busters, it might be helpful for us to know something of how they feel. For many Gen X'ers there is

A high level of distrust
Too much violence in the world
A searching for strong family units
A hunger for spiritual values
A lost sense of direction
A lost sense of hope

We in the Church Have a Faith to Share with the Busters

We share our faith because we want others to experience what we have experienced. However, before we actually share our faith with Busters, we will need to do the following:

❏ Understand their worldview.

❏ Demonstrate authentic love, for they are watching to see if we walk the talk.

❏ Demonstrate and embody a faith that works, which often means being open about our own doubts and struggles.

❏ Be authentic by being willing to be honest and to tell the truth.

❏ Demonstrate that Christianity is a relationship with a living person and not just another religion.

❏ Emphasize the sense of meaning and purpose that a relationship with Christ brings.

❏ Just tell the story and do not over-intellectualize the gospel.

❏ Assure them that not only does God love them, but God also values them as whole persons.

❏ Celebrate the awe and mystery of religion and ritual.

❏ Be a storyteller by linking your story to God's story.

❏ Do a lot of praying.

Keep These Thoughts in Mind When Sharing Your Faith with Busters

They are not looking for an orator but a communicator.

They are not looking for creeds or doctrine but relationships.

They are not looking for an institution but a community.

They have little or no denominational loyalty.

They have a consumer mentality when shopping for a church.

They are looking for that worshiping community that will nurture them spiritually while allowing them to stretch and grow.

They are looking for a sojourner, someone to journey with them.

They are thinkers who are feelers.

They are searching for how to experience truth.

They do not like labels.

They are used to language that is picturesque, graphic (remember, they have been influenced by MTV). They love the Old Testament because it is graphic and is filled with a struggle that is similar to their own experiences.

They do not want to *know* about God; they want to *experience* God.

Sharing Your Faith with Builders and Boomers

While most of this chapter focuses on learning how to share our faith with persons in the Buster generation, I would remind us that there are many persons in the Builder and Boomer generations who are searching for spiritual meaning. Many of the persons in these two categories are "recovering" Roman Catholics, Lutherans, Baptists, and United Methodists. They may have been reared in the church, but for a variety of reasons, they may have wandered away from those early roots. Some of them have simply been turned off by the church. Others have been hurt by the church or by someone in the church. Others have allowed other aspects of secular life to become the center of their existence; therefore, causing them to grow away from the church.

The American scene is now like a missionary field, rich with prospects for the Christian faith. The faith you possess is one that many persons are looking for. Rarely will people outside the church seek you out and ask you about your spiritual journey. As faith sharers we need to take the initiative. It can begin by simply inviting someone to worship with you. Keep in mind most everyone is looking for meaning and purpose in their life. By inviting someone to church you open up the process whereby they can begin a new faith journey and you will have the privilege of walking that journey with them.

The Twenty-First-Century Church

"Offer Them Christ" is the motto of The Foundation for Evangelism. It is also the historic and primary purpose of the people called "Methodists." In June of 1998, Bishop Ernest A. Fitzgerald, president of the foundation, wrote in *Forward*:

> From the days of John Wesley, our central calling has been to offer Christ to people around the world. This was accomplished by our circuit riders and missionaries, who often, at great personal risk and sacrifice, went forth proclaiming the word of God and the saving grace of Jesus Christ.
>
> Our church became a powerful force in molding the religious and social fabric of our country. We are not, however, reaching and impacting our world as we once did. According to a recent conversation with [nationally know evangelism leader] Eddie Fox, the United Methodist Church is presently losing the equivalent of a thousand-member congregation each week![2]

According to George Barna, thirty years ago there were 11.4 million members of the the United Methodist Church. Today there about 8.4 million members. Thirty years ago we have 4.5 million people in Sunday School, today that number is 2.0 million. In 1958, we lost 81,000 members to death. In 1988, we lost 127,000 members to death. We are not just a declining denomination; we are a dying denomination. People are not leaving us for other churches; they are moving on to The Church Triumphant!

I do not offer these disturbing statistics in the spirit of doom and gloom, but rather to excite us about the possibility of recovering our heritage as a Methodist movement as we move into the third millennium. There are many indications that this downward trend is changing. A part of the reason for this is because United Methodism is once again focusing its energies and resources on winning persons to Christ. There are many Builders, Boomers, as well as Busters in our society, who are waiting for us to "offer them Christ."

All of us share some common characteristics. We want to be loved and valued as a human being. Those of us who are privileged to be part of a Christian fellowship know that we are loved and valued because of our relationship with Jesus Christ. There are thousands of people who are just waiting for someone to tell them the good news. You have the story that many are waiting to hear and that our world desperately needs to hear. To all who come your way, offer them Christ!

Discussion Questions

1. Do you feel that sharing your faith to a Builder or a Boomer might be different from sharing your faith with a Buster? If so, how?

2. Have you seen an increase in attendance of Boomers and Busters in your church?

3. Look at your order of worship. Does it assume that persons attending the worship service have a general knowledge of what is happening? What could your church do to make your worship service more "user friendly"?

4. Do you feel that your church is positioned to minister to the Busters?

5. Do you feel that United Methodism has lost its evangelistic fervor?

6. Share one experience you have had in sharing your faith with another person.

7. If you are in the Builder or Boomer category, role-play how you would share your faith with someone who is in the Buster category.

8. What do you feel was Jesus' witness to the woman at the well?

Guideline # 6
*Invite persons to make a decision
today, for there may never be a
better day to begin following Jesus.*

Chapter 6

When God Says "Go," Go!

Acts 8:26-40

THE STORY OF Philip and his encounter with an Ethiopian eunuch is one of the most incredible stories you will find anywhere in the Bible. It is the story of a Jewish layperson baptizing a sexually challenged Black person somewhere along a road south of Jerusalem.

We do not know a great deal about Philip. He may or may not have been one of the twelve apostles. We do know that he was one of the seven deacons elected to a post in the Jerusalem church. We also know that he was an enthusiastic Christian. He was on fire with the life and message of Christ. If we are going to share our faith, then let it be done with enthusiasm.

Baron Von Hugel was once explaining the four conditions required for sainthood in the Roman Catholic Church. They are: loyalty to faith, heroism, endowment with powers beyond the usual, and a flaming radiance. Von Hugel then said, "The Roman Catholic Church may possibly be wrong

71

about the first three, but they are gloriously right about the fourth . . . a saint must be afire with radiance."[1]

Early Methodism understood this concept as well. John Wesley was once asked why people came to hear him preach. He could only say, "I really don't know. All I know is that the Spirit sets me on fire, and people come to watch me burn!"[2]

Did you know that the early Christians after the first Pentecost were called "The Burning Bunch"? Elton Trueblood often referred to the church as "The Incendiary Fellowship." Would people use such an image to describe a congregation at worship today? The word *enthusiasm* means "God in us." If God is in us, then the radiance of God ought to fill us and reflect itself in our very being.

Philip was on fire with the life and message of Christ. Whatever it was that Philip said to the eunuch, it burned its way deep into that African's heart so much so that something happened in him and he yielded his life to Christ— right there on the spot—and asked to receive baptism.

This remarkable story has a powerful message for persons desiring to share their faith.

Consider What Philip Found

The Ethiopian eunuch was a high official in the North African state, referred to in the Bible as Ethiopia. However, that region is probably not what we call Ethiopia today.

The eunuch was secretary of the treasury. Specifically, he was a court official of the queen's cabinet, in charge of her entire treasury. It was a common practice in those days for males placed in such positions of responsibility to be made into eunuchs. These men were often very intelligent persons with property and prominence.

The Bible tells us that this particular eunuch had been to Jerusalem to worship. He was not Jewish, but a he was a "believer." There were many such persons. They "believed" in the tenant of Judaism, but they did not formally become Jewish. This eunuch leaned in that direction.

We have a lot of "leaners" today. We have a lot of people who believe in God, that is to say, they lean toward God. Occasionally, a Gallup poll reminds us that eighty percent of Americans believe in God. That statistic sounds good until we discover how many of the eighty percent actually practice their religious beliefs in any formal way. It is then that we discover that many of the people who say they believe are persons who "lean" toward God, but do not get too close to God.

There is another poll that often causes United Methodists to get puffed up with pride. People who do not attend church are asked, "If you were to attend, which church would it be?" We are always pleased to hear that the majority of the people say they would attend a United Methodist church. We are comforted by this news. But again the results of the poll emphasize that people "lean" toward the church, but do not get too close.

The eunuch leaned toward Judaism because that was all he could do. However, the law of Judaism prevented eunuchs from becoming Jewish. The eunuch had obviously come to Jerusalem looking for meaning. He was not just another rush-hour commuter on his way home.

What Philip found was a man who was seeking something diligently, sincerely, and earnestly. The eunuch was not satisfied; he was reaching out for something more than he had ever known before. Although he had read the Scriptures, he longed to know their meaning as he looked for some turning point in his life. The eunuch knew his limitation to understanding; he knew he was an outsider looking in.

Could we use the same description for many in our world today? We have many persons searching for values, traditions, ethics, and morals, and that search takes many different forms. Prior to our moving to Minneapolis, there was a survey taken in our general geographic area. Hennepin Avenue United Methodist Church is located along a corridor from downtown to uptown, the most densely populated part of the Twin Cities. The survey revealed that nearly ninety percent of the persons interviewed indicated that they were searching for a spiritual life; yet eighty percent of those persons said that it would never occur to them to look to the church for their spirituality. This fits what John Naisbitt and Patricia Aburdene were telling us in their book, *Megatrends 2000*. They indicated that as we approach the new millennium, we will hear "yes" to spirituality and "no" to organized religion. Many of these persons are finding their "spirituality" completely outside the realm of traditional religion, such as in New Age religions, and yet they are all searching for a meaningful existence.[3]

Philip found such a person in the eunuch. He was searching, looking, and hoping to find something of value and meaning for his life. The significance of this story is that it may enable each of us to ask the difficult questions: Who are the eunuchs along the road of life? Who are the women and men and youth of today who seek to be whole in a fractured world? Who are the people in our society who yearn for refreshing streams of spiritual enlightenment? Who are the people who are limited by circumstances, yet yearn for a fuller participation in society?

What did Philip find? He found someone who was searching; someone who was hungry for meaning, someone who was waiting for some encouraging word of hope.

Consider What Philip Did

Philip preached to the eunuch. That is to say, he shared his faith. There are really only two ways to spread Christianity. One is to live our faith by example so that peo-

74

ple can see our faith by our deeds. The other way is to share our faith by telling people the story. This book focuses primarily on the latter.

The eunuch was reading Isaiah 53 when Philip asked him if he knew what he was reading. "No, not exactly," said the eunuch. Philip knew that the story needed interpretation.

Bishop Kenneth Goodson told a wonderful story about Dr. Merton Rice, one of the great preachers of an earlier generation. Dr. Rice would preach in his own church on Sunday mornings and then would travel to speak somewhere during the week. One night he arrived in Lima, Ohio, to preach in the coliseum. As he arrived he was pleased to see so many people pouring into the coliseum. However, Dr. Rice was a bit puzzled when he was asked for a ticket before entering. He was quite impressed with the fact that they sold tickets to come hear him. Dr. Rice explained who he was, and said that a ticket would not be necessary. He was politely told that they did not know anything about a Dr. Rice speaking, but that if he wanted to get in to hear Eugene Ormandy and the Philadelphia Symphony, he would need a ticket. As it turned out, Dr. Rice was one week early for his preaching assignment. So he bought a ticket and attended the concert.

Dr. Rice found himself sitting next to a man whose gaze was fixed on the stage. Dr. Rice, who was more at home with The Grand Ole Opry than the symphony, asked the man sitting next to him to explain what was happening on the stage. The man said he did not know because he was blind. As their conversation continued, the blind man said, "You don't know much about music, do you?" Dr. Rice admitted that he did not. The blind man said that he taught in the Cincinnati Conservatory. Then he said, "I'll make a deal with you. You tell me what is going on and I will interpret for you the depth of its meaning." It is said that the following Sunday, Dr. Rice preached one of the most profound sermons of his career. It was titled: "Life's Need for Interpretation."

There are a lot of folks around us who, like the eunuch, might appreciate a little interpretation of our faith. That does not always come easily for some Christians. We are willing to tell most anyone who our physician is. We tell people which hospital we go to and where we do our banking. All of these are rather personal issues, really. And yet, when it comes to our faith, we are sometimes curiously quiet. There may be many reasons for this silence. One may be that we are just not confident enough in our own faith to share it with anyone. Another reason may be that we do not know how to share our faith. There are others who feel that one's personal faith is a private matter, not to be shared with others. We also know that there are persons who are just turned off by the way some folks have tried to share their faith.

Our faith is something to be shared. Some years ago there was a college student who became a Christian. He had taken a summer job working in a logging camp. This choice of occupation concerned some of his new Christian friends. They felt that the worldly lumberjacks might tease him and perhaps tempt him to let go of his faith.

When the summer was over the young man returned to school. "What was it like?" his friends wanted to know. "Did you make it O.K.? Was it difficult for you? Did the lumberjacks give you a bad time because of your faith?" "Oh, no," he responded. "There weren't any problems at all. You see they never found out that I was a Christian!"

Unfortunately, that is the way it is with too many of us Christians. We remain silent about our faith. But more and more we are being surrounded by persons who are searching for a faith that will give them meaning and purpose for living. These persons would appreciate a little interpretation of what the Christian faith is all about.

Philip asked the eunuch, "Do you understand what you are reading?" The eunuch answered, "How can I understand unless someone guides me?" Philip became the guide. You may discover a variety of opportunities of how you can become a guide.

Many years ago there was a Presbyterian minister who served a large church in an industrial city. The most active and generous person in his church was a woman who was married to one of the most prominent and wealthy men in the city. Her husband, however, never attended, nor gave to, the church.

The pastor of the church decided to pay a visit to the woman's husband at his office. The pastor had rehearsed what he wanted to say, but was still somewhat intimidated when he was ushered into the man's great office and found this older gentleman seated behind a massive desk.

The pastor sat in front of him and proceeded with his story. When he finished he was greeted with dead silence. The man never spoke a word. Feeling uneasy, the pastor tried to retell what was weighing so heavily on his mind. Again, nothing but silence from the other side of the desk.

At that point the pastor wished he had never made that appointment and was looking for a quick way out of the office, when the man reached for a pad and wrote something on it. He passed it to the minister. The note read, "I am so deeply moved that I cannot speak."

Later the man told the pastor that his visit was the first time an adult, in a frank, straightforward way, had ever discussed with him the Christian gospel. According to the story the man did indeed become a member of the church and became one of the great Christian leaders in the city.

What did Philip do? He told the story.

Consider What Happened

Because Philip followed the direction of the Spirit by traveling to some unknown spot on the highway, and interpreted the Scriptures, the eunuch asked to be baptized.

In reality, however, the outcome is even more exciting. Tradition has it that the eunuch was not only responsible for the Christian conversion and baptism of the queen, but was also responsible for bringing Christianity to Ethiopia.

If you have visited Jerusalem you may have visited the Church of the Holy Sepulcher. This is the place believed to be where Jesus was crucified and buried. The Church of the Holy Sepulcher is a strange mixture of Russian Orthodox, Eastern Orthodox, and Roman Catholic influences. The Ethiopians were not permitted to have an altar in this sacred place; however, they were granted a spot up on the roof of the church.

The chapel is about the size of a large bathroom, and it is where the bishop of the Coptic Church resides. What makes this place so special is that historians believe that it was the first church in Christendom. Today there are millions of Christians in Ethiopia. They have kept their faith through wars, persecution, poverty, and oppression. In fact, they have experienced phenomenal growth as a result of these reversals.

Historians tell us that all these events began with the eunuch and Philip, a man willing to follow the Spirit of God. While the outcome may not always be quite this dramatic, the point is well made. When we respond to what God is calling us to do by sharing our faith, a powerful transformation may take place.

Philip left Jerusalem and went out into the middle of the desert, to an intersection, he knew not where. He then stood at noon in the heat of the sun to meet someone he did not yet know. Philip climbed into the eunuch's chariot and talked to him about Jesus, which led the eunuch to make a commitment that not only transformed his life but the life of an entire nation.

How about you? Are you a Philip to those around you? Are you bearing witness to your faith in Jesus Christ? Your response to the leading of the Spirit in your life could very well alter your destiny as well as the course of history.

"And the Spirit of the Lord revealed to Philip, 'Arise, Philip, and go,' and he went." I do not know what this means to you, but for me it means that if God says, "Go," then go!

Discussion Questions

1 Do you feel that most people would be comfortable with the notion that the radiance of God ought to be reflected in our very being? If so, why?

2. Do you think that the word *spirituality* means different things to different people? If so, how would your view of spirituality differ from someone who was a Gen-Xer?

3. Spend some time discussing where you think some persons search for their spirituality if not in the church.

4. List some reasons why you feel some Christians seek to keep their Christian faith a secret.

5. Have you ever taken the initiative to ask someone to make a decision for Christ? If so, how did that go?

6. Share with the group how you bear witness to the presence of Christ in your life.

Guideline # 7
*Do not give up on people because
they do not become believers on
your time schedule.*

Chapter 7

Join Wait Watchers

Exodus 24:12-18

OVER THE COURSE of your lifetime, you will spend at least five years waiting in lines, two years just trying to get in touch with people by telephone, eight months opening nothing but junk mail, and six months waiting for the traffic light to turn green. In order to get to work, the average time we spend behind the steering wheel is about sixty minutes a day. This means that you will spend six forty-hour work weeks just getting yourself to and from work.[1] A tremendous amount of your life is spent just waiting.

The subject of waiting is quite common in the Bible. The word *wait* appears 106 times in the Bible. In Exodus 24:12, we read the following: "The Lord said to Moses, 'Come up to me on the mountain, and wait there; and I will give you the tables of stone, with the law and the commandment, which I have written for their instruction.'" We have come to know that these "instructions" were written by the finger of God and are what we call the Ten Commandments.

The stage is now set for a unique event and encounter. Moses leaves the people and instructs Aaron to oversee them in his absence. He then takes Joshua, his personal servant, and the two of them begin to ascend the mountain. However, about halfway up, Moses announces that God has called him to go to the top alone. The scene is most dramatic. A mysterious cloud engulfs the mountain. Moses waits in this cloud for six days. That is a long time to be alone on top of a mountain immersed in a cloud. It is a long time to wait, especially if you do not know why you are waiting.

Finally, the voice of the Almighty echoes in the midst of the cloud, and suddenly, the presence of God becomes a fire on top of the mountain, a fire so great that the folks at the foot of the mountain are able to see the flames. There, in that dramatic moment, the story comes to an end. Now, that is a lot of waiting. Maybe that is what "keep the faith" means—being faithful when nothing much seems to be happening. There, for six long days, Moses experienced nothing. Six days of nothing!

How different this story would have been if Moses, instead of sticking it out until the seventh day, would have given up and retreated down the mountain to join the people. I can imagine there must have been moments during that long waiting period on top of the mountain when Moses might have cried out, "God, what is it that you want?" Moses was not the most patient person in the world. I can clearly imagine him saying somewhere along the fifth or sixth day, "God, if something doesn't happen here soon, I'm out of here!"

But no, despite the hardships, the swirling clouds, and the sense that one was encamped on the edge of a devouring fire, Moses stuck it out. His experience taught him that if he wanted to hear God's voice, he had to be willing to wait. Because of his obedience, he finally did experience God's glory on top of that mountain.

Moses' experience is helpful to us. How do you handle life when nothing seems to be happening? You have prayed for something to happen, but it does not. You have asked God for help, and it seems as though the prayer is not heard. Is God not there? Does God not care, or is God just too busy to listen?

So much of life is waiting. We wait for a doctor's report regarding our health; we wait for a troubled teenager to "come home"; we wait to hear about our future with the corporation; as elderly parents wait to hear from an estranged son or daughter. Most of us do not do very well when we have to wait, especially when it seems as though nothing is happening.

An article in *Newsweek* entitled "The Day the Beepers Died" proves that fact as it told about that fateful day when the beepers went silent. Talk about nothing happening! By the end of the week, most of the beepers were once again beeping. The brief bout of chaos was a sign of how dependent we have become on all our high-tech info-infrastructure gizmos.[2]

The really scary thing was that no one anticipated such a meltdown in the first place. The culprit was the Galaxy IV, a five-year-old communications satellite hovering some 22,300 miles over Kansas. The $250 million satellite is just a nine-foot cube with two fifty-foot solar-panel wings, but it has a "footprint" covering the United States and the Caribbean.

Apparently, the onboard computer that keeps the satellite pointed at the Earth failed and so did the backup. The result? Some 45 million pagers went dead. When it failed, all the physicians, police officers, business people and worried parents were suddenly incommunicado. But that wasn't the extent of the problem. Gas stations lost the ability to take credit cards at the pump, and National Public Radio winked out along with several airlines canceling flights while waiting for information regarding altitude, weather reports, and radar.

If waiting is difficult for you, especially if you are waiting for some kind of sign or response, let me suggest that you join Wait Watchers. The organization has not yet been organized, but I'm working on it. I'm looking for a few charter members who will strive to have a new way of looking at the business of patient waiting.

When nothing happens, wait! God may be teaching you patience so that you can trust what God is doing. Let us always remember that our God is a waiting God. This is evidenced by the story of the transfiguration of Jesus as recorded in the Gospel of Matthew (17:1-9). Jesus took three of his closest disciples—James, John, and Peter—up on a mountain, and there before their very eyes, they saw Jesus transfigured into dazzling white and flanked on either side by Moses and Elijah.

Frightened by the experience the disciples fell to the ground, only to be reassured a few moments later by Jesus who told them not to be afraid. James, John, and Peter wanted to build three monuments up on that mountain so no one would forget what had just happened. But Jesus discouraged them from doing that and, moreover, instructed them to tell no one about what they had seen until certain conditions were ready.

God indeed is a waiting God. This waiting reminds us that God does not operate within the parameters of our calendars or our clocks. God's sense of time is something quite different from ours.

This is important for us to keep in mind when we get so caught up in our own timelines and agendas. A great preacher of another generation, Phillips Brooks, was pacing back and forth one day in a terrible fit of agitation. Finally, a friend asked him what was wrong, and Brooks replied, "I'm in a hurry, but God is not!" Things are happening even when we think nothing is happening.

One of my friends, now retired, is one of the distinguished preachers of this country, Dr. Ben Garrison. Several years ago, I received his church letter in which his announced the sermon topic for the following Sunday was "A Crockpot Faith for a Microwave World." That says it all. We want everything so fast. We are looking for the computer that can boast ZERO WAITING! But things of God take time, and when we think nothing is happening, we are often wrong, for something may be happening. We just may not be aware of what that is.

When nothing is happening, wait! There are two kinds of waiting. There is passive waiting in which one does virtually nothing. This kind of waiting is found in the delightful story about a duke and duchess who wanted to review the employment of their servant, Hobbs. The duchess said to Hobbs, "I see by our records that you have been in our employ for 35 years." Hobbs said, "That is correct, Ma'am." "Well, Hobbs," said the duchess, "what has been your primary responsibility during those years?" Hobbs replied, "Taking care of the family dog." The duchess said, "Well, Hobbs, according to our records, the family dog died 27 years ago." "Yes, Ma'am," said Hobbs, "and I would like to know what you would like to have me do now."

The second is waiting with a sense of anticipation, realizing that even in our moments of waiting, God is at work and something is happening. This active waiting is biblical because it is based on trusting God even when it appears to us that nothing is happening.

This is the kind of waiting that might be involved whenever we share our faith with someone. Just because we have told our story does not mean the listener will be ready to commit. Just because we have given a well-crafted witness to someone does not mean that he or she will show up in church the next Sunday. Our task is to share our faith, to plant the seed, if you will, and then to nurture and care for that seed in ways that hopefully will produce results. But we are not alone in this process. We are simply agents of the Holy Spirit. We may think that nothing is happening, but more may be happening than we realize. By sharing your faith, you make it possible for God to work within that person. You may see the results of your witness, or you may not. Do not give up on someone because they do not become a believer on your time schedule. Continue to share your faith when appropriate and hold on to them in prayer. When we are faithful in our witness, the mystery of God's spirit is able to work.

Be willing to do the kind of waiting that was done by the great Colonial pastor Cotton Mather, who prayed for a revival several hours a day for twenty years. The Great Awakening for which he prayed began the year he died. The same kind of waiting brought about the abolishment of slavery in the British Empire as a result of the Christian parliamentarian and abolitionist leader William Wilberforce, who lay on his deathbed exhausted from his nearly fifty-year campaign against the practice of human bondage. Hudson Taylor devoted his life as a missionary in the Orient, and during his lifetime he witnessed few conversions. Today, however, millions of Chinese embrace the Christian faith which Taylor so patiently planted and tended.[2]

I think of other missionaries like William Carey, missionary to India; Judson, missionary to Burma; Robert Morrison, medical missionary to China; and David Livingston, missionary/explorer—all of whom served in their various areas for upwards of 15 years before ever receiving their first convert.

I think of persons like Adam Clark, who spent forty years writing his commentary on the Scriptures. Noah Webster worked thirty-six years on his dictionary, crossing the ocean twice to collect material. William Cullan Bryant wrote *Thanatopsis* one hundred times before he was satisfied with the finished product. Charles Goodyear worked in poverty and ridicule perfecting rubber before it could be made into a tire, and George Stevenson worked for fifteen long years developing the locomotive.

We may think nothing is happening, but that simply is not the case. In what appears to be nothingness, God is actively involved and much is happening. Our task is to join Wait Watchers. It doesn't mean sitting around and doing nothing, but it does mean having the patience to trust that God is at work in our lives and in our world.

Join Wait Watchers! You can sign up right now.

Discussion Questions

1. What makes waiting difficult for you?

2. Would you be willing to wait like Moses did if you were unable to know why you were waiting?

3. What do you think was the reason why Moses waited it out on that mountain?

4. Do you feel uncomfortable when nothing seems to be happening? Do you feel the need to make something happen is nothing is happening?

5. Does waiting make you anxious?

6. What have you learned about the value of patience and waiting?

Chapter 8

Shout and Sing for Joy!

Luke 10:1-19

SEVERAL YEARS AGO an article appeared in a local newspaper about a woman and her pet parakeet named Chippy. Apparently the woman decided to clean the bottom of Chippy's birdcage with a canister vacuum while Chippy remained in the cage. When the phone rang, the woman turned to pick up the receiver and just as she did she heard the horrible sound of Chippy being sucked into the vacuum.

She dropped the receiver, tore open the canister, and dumped the contents of fluff and filth onto the floor. Out dropped Chippy. If all of this had not been traumatic enough, she picked up the little bird, ran out to the kitchen, and proceeded to wash off Chippy under the kitchen faucet.

Some time later an enterprising newspaper reporter heard of the incident and came out to see the woman to get the story. After listening to her tale of woe, the reporter asked, "Tell me, how is Chippy doing?" The woman replied, "Well,

Chippy isn't so chipper these days. He doesn't sing much any more. He just sits and stares."

Over the last forty years I have preached to a lot of people who feel like that. Little wonder. Each day we deal with such huge issues such as domestic violence, child abuse, drug and alcohol abuse, global hunger, breakdown in relationships, White House scandals, pollution, senseless acts of violence, conflicts in the Middle East or the Balkans, dealing with loved ones who are HIV positive.... The list goes on and on. We don't sing much any more. We just sit and stare.

This is not a unique problem. The entire Bible is a record of troubled times with persons struggling for survival and searching for meaning. One of the darkest periods of history in the Hebrew Scriptures was during the Exile. Many of the Israelites were pulled away from their homes and families and taken to Babylon. These folks did not sing much. They just sat and stared. But in the midst of that hopelessness, the people heard the prophet Isaiah boldly proclaim, "Sing praises to the LORD, for he has done gloriously;/let this be known in all the earth./Shout and sing for joy, O royal Zion,/for great in your midst is the Holy One of Israel" (Isaiah 12:5-6).

This is one of the greatest affirmations of hope found anywhere in the Bible. Isaiah is telling us that we can shout and sing for joy, for even in the midst of our misery, God is in our midst. Notice how God came in the midst of fear and turmoil and the dark of night when Christ was born. Notice how God broke into the darkness of death and despair on that first Easter morn. Notice how God once again broke into the midst of timidity and uncertainty on that first Pentecost, transforming those distraught, directionless disciples into a powerful band of witnesses who literally turned the world upside down.

The task for the new millennial Christian is quite clear. We are called by God to witness to the truth that God through Christ is indeed in our midst. If we do not share that good news with others, who will? The apostle Paul put it very well in his letter to the Romans: "And how are they to believe in one of whom they have never heard? And how are they to hear without someone to proclaim him? And how are they to proclaim him unless they are sent? As it is written, 'How beautiful are the feet of those who bring good news!'" (Romans 10:14-15).

We are surrounded each day by vast numbers of people who hunger for the faith we have. What a joy and privilege it is for us to share our faith. In this closing chapter, I want to discuss with you what is involved in witnessing to our faith. Two thoughts are important: first, that each and every one of us sense that we have been called by God to share our faith in one way or another; second, that God will empower us to fulfill that task. "But you will receive power when the Holy Spirit has come upon you; and you will be my witnesses in Jerusalem, in all Judea and Samaria, and to the ends of the earth" (Acts 1:8).

No doubt the greatest single reason why some folks are reluctant to share their faith is because they feel inadequate in articulating it. However, if we truly believe that we have been called by God to share our faith, then we will know something of the power of the Holy Spirit, which will help us in this venture. As ambassadors of the good news, we look to opportunities to share with others how God's love has been experienced in our lives and how we have experienced God breaking into our darkness and despair.

For too many years we in the church have left this to the "professionals," like ordained clergy. We are seeing a significant change in this approach, with many churches training and equipping the laity to share their faith. Most persons outside the faith would expect an ordained elder or an ordained deacon to share their faith. Some of the most meaningful faith sharing taking place today is being done, not by the professionals, but by persons who are willing to tell someone else how God has moved in their life.

The men and women whom Jesus dispatched were not trained religious professionals. They were common ordinary folk who made their living in the world. They were the ones who fished and repaired nets and boats. They were merchants, laborers, tent makers, tax collectors, accountants, and bookkeepers, as well as government officials. In every instance these common men and women were willing to tell the story and to share their faith.

Why Does the Christian Bear Witness?

People are searching for meaning and purpose in life. Christianity is more than a set of abstract principles based on first-century thinking. It is a message of ultimate importance addressing the deeper issues of life.

Because we have experienced God's redemptive love and grace, we have this burning desire to share that reality with others. This is what the Great Commission in the closing verses of Matthew is all about. Christ calls us to go out into the world and witness to the powerful truth of the Gospel.

In one of my early sermons at the beginning of my ministry at Trinity United Methodist Church in Lincoln, NE, I quoted Nebraska's poet laureate, the late Dr. John Neihart. Following the worship service, a member of the congregation introduced herself to me by saying that she typed manuscripts for Dr. Neihart and wondered if I would like to meet him sometime. Well, of course, I was thrilled with that prospect.

It wasn't long before I was ushered into the poet's presence, with my friend saying, "Dr. Neihart, I want you to meet my minister, Dr. Rod Wilmoth." He graciously acknowledged my presence and then said, "Now, what did

Florence say that you do?" "I am her pastor", I said. "Oh,"
exclaimed Dr. Neihardt, "how lucky you are! You have the
honor of being a storyteller." I said, "Well, Dr. Neihart, that
is true. But you are the gifted storyteller with your books
and poetry." "Oh, yes," he said, "I know. But I tell stories
about people and places in history. You, on the other hand,
have been given the honor of telling *the* story—the story that
is truly the hope of the world."

Why do we bear witness to our faith? Hopefully not
because we are mandated to do so, but because we want to.
We do so because we have personally experienced God's
redemptive love and grace and want to share that good news
with persons who may be searching for words of hope.

To What Does the Christian Bear Witness?

The Christian life speaks of human possibilities when
lived in relationship to God. It lifts the human enterprise so
that people can see themselves in a new way and in a new
light. To that end we witness to:

To a Living God

A little girl wrote the following note: "Dear God: How do
you feel about people who do not believe in you?" She
signed her name and then added this postscript: "Someone
else wants to know." Most of us could write such a note
regardless of our age. Sometimes even the most faithful wonder about the existence of God.

Many years ago a rich widow of New York City died and
left a sizable estate to God. Her strange bequest gave rise to
the legal entanglements. In order to settle the estate, the
lawyers in the case made certain that the proper procedures
were followed to the letter. They prepared a lawsuit which

named God as one of the parties. A summons was issued requiring God to file a legal response. The summons was delivered to the sheriff, whose responsibility was to serve the papers. When the sheriff's final report was delivered to the court, it read, "After due and diligent search, it has been determined that God cannot be found in New York City."[1]

The good news that we bring in sharing our faith is the witness to a living God who is alive and well and is in our midst. Our God is not some static thought, but is a living presence. It may be that some folks have not seen God because they are looking in all the wrong places. We would do well to remember that God comes to us in unlikely ways and places. Let us bear witness to a living God.

To a New Life in Christ

We witness the fact that lives have been changed and new beginnings have been made possible. The bondage of fear, emptiness and brokenness have given way to courage, meaning and wholeness. New life in Christ is not an achievement; it is a gift.

The radical change that can take place in our lives does so when we realize that God loves us unconditionally. This is wonderfully seen in the life experiences of some of the great notables of the New Testament. For example, there is the apostle Peter, who was more of a sand pile than a rock—a man who denied even knowing the one who loved him the most. And then there was Zacchaeus, the little rich man who had to climb a tree in order to get a glimpse of Jesus. Remember that he is the one who agreed to exhort taxes from his own people for the Roman government so that he could get a "kick back" from the take. And then there was Mary Magdalene, the prostitute, and James and John, a couple of "Momma's boys" who kept arguing who was the greatest. And don't forget Thomas, the doubter, and the two men on the crosses beside Jesus, a thief and a convicted criminal.

But then look at what happened to these people. They experienced new life in Christ. Through Christ, God was able to love and accept them unconditionally, thus elevating the level of their life. Peter, the "sand pile," ultimately became the "rock" who would not move in his dedication to the cause of Christ, even in the face of death. Zacchaeus, the corrupt tax collector, became a champion of the poor, and Mary Magdalene, a woman of questionable reputation, became a woman who stood weeping outside the tomb of Jesus. The apostles James and John became true followers of Christ, proclaiming the good news of God's unconditional love wherever they traveled. Let us likewise bear witness to the living Christ.

To a Creative and Redemptive Fellowship

When Methodism was merely a movement in England in the days of John Wesley, it was characterized by social action and concern for others. The early mothers and fathers of the movement established schools and organized corps of visitors who moved among the poor and the sick. They organized a "war on poverty" long before our government made it fashionable. They attacked slavery and were among the most outspoken advocates for civil liberty and social justice.

These early Methodists did more than "gather together to ask the Lord's blessing and to sing praises to God's name." They operated their missions and were the dissenting, protesting reformers of society, seeking to be the Christian presence through the church. This is our rich heritage which comes out of our Wesleyan tradition. Many of the persons who are searching for a meaningful faith today are looking for just such a community where they can put their new faith and beliefs into action. We will never have a better opportunity than right now to bear witness to the creative and redemptive fellowship of the church.

How Does the Christian Bear Witness?

There are different approaches and styles. Bill Hybels, senior pastor of Willow Creek Community Church in South Barrington, Ill., along with Mark Mittelbergt, evangelism trainer at that church, have written a book entitled *Becoming A Contagious Christian*. One of the chapters is called "Finding the Approach That Fits You." I share some of their approaches of witnessing for consideration. Obviously the point is to find the approach that truly fits who you are. Your approach may be one or more of the following.

Peter's Confrontational Approach

Peter was certainly not known for his finesse. Peter is often described as a "ready-fire-aim" kind of guy. There is a profound beauty and power in Peter. He minces no words. For him Jesus is the Messiah. He is quick and impulsive, argumentative and combative. Such an approach may work for some but not for others. Knowing your audience is critically important in choosing the approach we want to use when it comes time to share our faith with someone.

Paul's Intellectual Approach

Paul could confront along with the best, but his approach was to reason. Paul was highly educated and a great teacher. He was well equipped to take on the philosophers in Athens. In his teaching we see how Paul has a natural tendency to argue point-counterpoint with imaginary foes who might challenge his position. There will be times when this will be the best approach.

Blind Beggar's Approach

This incredible story is recorded in the 9th chapter of John. Here a blind beggar receives the healing touch of

Christ, and his sight is restored. All kinds of issues were raised with this miracle. Was the man blind because of the sin of his parents or his own sin? Was he really blind? Through it all, it is the blind person who says, "One thing I do know. I was blind but now I see." John tells us that when the blind man found out it was Jesus who restored his eyesight, he not only believed but he also followed.

Matthew's Interpersonal Approach

A tax collector turned evangelist makes for a strange combination, and yet this is exactly what happened when Matthew received the call to follow Jesus. Matthew's approach was quite different from the others. He did not confront nor intellectually challenge anyone, nor is there any evidence that he tells anyone of what happened to him. Rather, he moved about caring for persons in his own way by reaching out in friendship, influencing persons to consider the claims of Christ.

Samaritan Woman's Invitational Approach

God chooses unlikely people to touch the lives of others. Here is a woman who had three strikes against her: she was living in a questionable situation, she was a woman, and she was a Samaritan. But that did not stop Jesus because he saw value in her and dignity as a human being. Convinced that Jesus was the Messiah, this woman immediately goes to her town and brings a group of people back to the well to hear and experience the Christ.

Think about what your witness could mean to the lost, the lonely, and the least.

Dorcas' Service Approach

The Bible tells us that Dorcas was "devoted to good works and acts of charity" (Acts 9:36). She was well known for her

97

loving acts of service which she performed in the name of Christ. Her approach to witnessing was through service. Perhaps that is why there are so many Dorcas Circles in United Methodist Women. They are typical of our United Methodist heritage, which stresses both holiness and social action.

The Best Approach is Your Approach

You will want to witness to your faith in a way that is authentic to your experience. Whatever approach you use must be sincere and from your heart. Only then will it be convincing and helpful to others.

Where Does the Christian Bear Witness?

The Christian bears witness wherever and whenever the situation presents itself.

All of this brings us back to both the desire on our part to share our faith and need for persons to share their faith. Too many of us are like the young person who was afraid to tell his lumberjack friends that he was a Christian for fear they would ridicule him.

This may be a part of the problem in sharing our faith. Too many are what I call "Undercover Christians." They are so secretive about their faith that no one knows they are Christians in the first place.

The Christian faith is meant for us to accept, absorb, and then pass on to others. It is only in the passing on of the faith that the story of God's love, grace, forgiveness, and redemption lives on and becomes real to the many people who long to have a faith like ours.

In Luke's account, Jesus sends out the seventy with a sense of urgency to share their faith. He warned them that they would not always be welcome. All they really had was the promise that Jesus would be with them. The seventy dispersed and in time returned. They must have been quite excited because they reported to Jesus that people did indeed listen to their story. Jesus said that at that moment, "I watched Satan fall" (10:18). Each of us today is sent out to share our faith.

An outdoor symphony concert was scheduled in an American city, and the guest conductor was the symphony director in one of the opera houses in Bavaria. The conductor had come to the United States on a recruiting trip and had agreed to conduct that city's orchestra as a favor to a former student.

The concert was in the city's baseball stadium, and unfortunately, because of a schedule mix up, a slow-pitch softball game was taking place on an adjoining field. The audience sitting in the stands could see the game going on, and, worse yet, they could hear everything over the public address system. The first part of the concert was a disaster. The soothing sounds of Respighi's "The Pines of Rome" were interspersed with "The next batter for Schultz's Bar is Billy Ray." That would be followed by loud voices shouting, "Give 'er a ride, Billy Ray!" The symphony players were unnerved and misplayed some sections of the work, and the regular conductor was visibly struggling simply to keep control.

The orchestra finally struggled to intermission, wondering if any of the crowd would return for the second part of the concert. The fame of the visiting Maestro Lehrer was such, however, that the stands were indeed full. Maestro Lehrer was introduced and mounted the podium to conduct the Sibelius tone-poem "Finlandia."

Just at that moment someone hit a home run over the fence and the softball crowd went wild. The Maestro merely waited until the noise subsided and then smiled at the orchestra. He raised his baton and began "Finlandia." A

magical change came over the whole scene. His command-
ing presence pulled the individual orchestra members
together into one ensemble, a focused fellowship. The
momentum increased; the orchestra outdid itself; the
Maestro was in total control, and as the great composition
reached its climax, members of the orchestra heard Lehrer
shouting, "Das ist der Geist! Das ist der Geist! (That's the
spirit! That's the spirit!)."

When the performance reached its vibrant conclusion,
the people jumped to their feet with thunderous applause.
At that moment something wonderful happened. The softball players had stopped their game to listen to the majestic
music, and when it was over, they too stood to their feet and
clapped.[2]

This is a powerful parable for our time. If we are faithful
in telling the story and sharing our faith, the world will stop
to listen, and we will see Satan fall.

Discussion Questions

1. Do you feel the church adequately prepares persons to
   share their faith? What could your church do to help
   persons share their faith?

2. Name some places where you could most effectively
   share your faith.

3. Do you feel the Great Commission in the Gospel of
   Matthew is still relevant today?

4. Give some examples of how you have shared your
   faith. How did the opportunity present itself, and what
   did you say? What was the result of your faith sharing?

5. How would you describe your "approach" to faith sharing?

6. What do you think would happen if everyone in our congregations took God's call seriously enough to share their faith with someone else?

Notes

Notes to Introduction

1. H. Eddie Fox and George E. Morris, *Faith-Sharing: Dynamic Christian Witnessing by Invitation*, Discipleship Resources.
2. Charles Yrigoyen, Jr., *John Wesley: Holiness of Heart and Life*, The Mission Education and Cultivation Program Department for the Women's Division General Board of Global Ministries, The United Methodist Church.
3. George Hunter III, "Top 10 Reasons for NOT Leaving Evangelism to the Pastor," *Circuit Rider*, February, 1997.

Notes to Chapter 1

1. *Journal*, May 24, 1738.
2. From a sermon preached by Clarence Forsberg, formerly of St. Paul UMC, Lincoln, NE.
3. *Pulpit Resource*, July, August, September, 1984.
4. *The Minister's Annual Manual*, October 19, 1997.

Notes to Chapter 2

1. H. Eddie Fox and George E. Morris, *Faith-Sharing: Dynamic Christian Witnessing by Invitation*, Disciple-ship Resources.
2. Harold W. Roberts, "Communion in a Divided World," *Pulpit Digest*, September/October 1985.
3. *Journal*, May 24, 1738.
4. *Dynamic Preaching*, July, August, September, 1998.

Notes to Chapter 3

1. *LectionAid,* January, February, March, 1997.
2. *Homiletics,* May, June, 1997.
3. Materials provided by Goodwill Industries.
4. Rev. Mark Trotter, First United Methodist Church, San Diego, California.

Notes to Chapter 4

1. Mark Trotter, First United Methodist Church, San Diego, California.

Notes to Chapter 5

1. Gary L. McIntosh, *Make Room for the Boom...or Bust: Six Models for Reaching Three Generations,* Net Results, March 1998.
2. Chart provided by the Gen X'er workshop at Robert Schuller Institute, January, 1999.
3. Bishop Ernest A. Fitzgerald, *Forward,* June, 1998.

Notes to Chapter 6

1. *Celebration,* June 1989.
2. Charles Yrigoyen, Jr. *John Wesley: Holiness of Heart and Life,* Women's Division of the General Board of Global Ministries.
3. *Religious Revival of the Third Millennium,* Chapter 9.

Notes to Chapter 7

1. Jeff Davidson, *The Complete Idiot's Guide to Managing Time,* New York: Alpha Books, 1995.
2. *Newsweek,* June 15, 1998.
3. Charles Colson, *Loving God,* Zondervan Publishing House.

Notes to Chapter 8

1. *Pulpit Digest,* September/October, 1987, page 15.
2. David F. Lehmberg, First UMC, Claremont, CA.